INSECURE ATTACHMENT

The search of emotional stability, tools to promote understanding and to lay the foundation for strong and healthy relationships

Table of contents

Introduction 1

Part I: Evaluation.. 3

Chapter 1: Insecure attachment decoded............................. 4

   Security in relationships.. 4

   Dismissive partners.. 6

   Preoccupied partners 8

   Disorganized partners... 9

Chapter 2: Showing poor attitude & suspicion 12

Chapter 3: Constant anxiety & depression 20

Chapter 4: Endless drama & obsessive disorder.................. 28

Chapter 5: Irresponsible behavior.. 36

Part II: Causes 45

Chapter 6: Childhood trauma 46

Chapter 7: Failure and rejection 54

Chapter 8: Negative people in your life................................ 62

Chapter 9: Low self-esteem.. 70

Chapter 10: Judgmental society 76

Part III: Overcoming 79

Chapter 11: Raising your self-awareness 80

Chapter 12: Raising your confidence levels 87

Chapter 13: Surrounding yourself with positive people 95

Chapter 14: Components of a healthy relationship.............. 99

Conclusion.. 106

Introduction

In a successful relationship, people need to be secure. This means they need to govern their emotions and habits in order to ensure a peaceful coexistence with their partner. Partners need to be well-adjusted in order they may have a healthy and rewarding relationship. But sadly, this cannot be said to be the case for many relationships. Partners that struggle with insecure attachment issues are virtually incapable of having healthy relationships. psychologists believe that insecure attachment begins in early childhood. The experiences of a child in relation to their parents and the surrounding environment are going to influence how they turn out as adults. When a child develops a healthy bond with the people in their early life, they become secure. This means they will have a positive attitude and expect the best from other people. Such kids grow to be stale partners who expect other people to play their part. But when a child has an unhealthy bond with their early life environment, such a kid is likely to grow up to exhibit insecure attachment, whereby they expect the worst of people. Such people end up becoming distrustful of others and it presents significant challenges in relationships. they are likely to be unpredictable. They won't show any consistency in their behaviors and actions. One moment they might act charged and interested and the next moment they might act withdrawn and disconnected, like a robot. Insecure attachment may be overcome but it requires the full participation of the affected person. This book delves into the subject of insecure attachment issues and makes suggestions on how to get rid of it.

Part I: Evaluation

Chapter 1:

Insecure attachment decoded

Relationships play a critical role in our happiness, but if the partners are not compatible, it can give rise to tremendous pain. One of the factors that would contribute to difficult relationships is the presence of insecure attachment issues in either or both partners. Generally, attachment issues stem from an individual's childhood experiences. If the child had a stable relationship with their parents, they developed a healthy bond with other human beings, and in later years when they get into a relationship, they will have a positive mindset and expect to rely on the other person. However, if someone had a negative relationship with their parent, they likely developed an unhealthy bond, and it makes it hard for them to trust their partners; these people will always be expecting their partners to do them in and this mindset usually sabotages the relationship.

Security in relationships

For a relationship to be healthy and withstand the test of time, both partners must be secure. These are some of the factors that point to security in a relationship:

- **Comfort**

Partners must be comfortable with one another. They must be looking to meet each other. In a scenario where the partners are uncomfortable with one another thy will be trying to get away from each other as they dread being together. Such a relationship usually continues because the involved people are scared of being alone.

- **Reliability**

In a healthy relationship, partners must be able to rely on each other. In a healthy relationship, both partners must work as a team. People who have no attachment issues are most likely to have a positive attitude towards depending other people and this causes them to do their part and expect that their partner will play their role too.

- **Respecting each other's space**

Just because you are in a relationship doesn't mean you should act as though you are joined with your partner at the hip. Both partners should give each other sufficient space, but the partners should have no problem with that. For someone with attachment issues, it is particularly hard to give their partner space because they are afraid of staying alone, and they want to cling onto their partner.

- **Forgiving**

In healthy relationships, partners must be forgiving toward each other. They must recognize that no one is without blame. And some of the mistakes that people make are not intentional. If there's no forgiveness in a relationship, it's likely to contribute to resentment toward each other, and this can ruin the relationship. But if there's forgiveness, it means that the partners will deepen their love toward each other, and the relationship will become even stronger.

- **Open communication**

When two emotionally healthy people get into a relationship, they cannot afford to go quiet on each other, but they will find ways to always communicate with each other. This keeps misunderstandings away and helps couples to grow close to one another.

- Empathy

In healthy relationships, partners are also in a position to be empathetic toward each other. This means they can understand what the other person is going through and make a point of helping out. In the absence of empathy, there's viciousness and it makes it hard to have a healthy relationship.

Dismissive partners

One of the types of people who demonstrate insecure attachment tend to be dismissive. And such behavior obviously makes it hard for people to have a healthy relationship. Some of the ways that the dismissive person will behave include:

- **Emotionally distant**

For a relationship to be stable, the partners need to be intimate. But then a dismissive person frustrates their partner by being emotionally distant. This makes their partner to become resentful and the relationship starts disintegrating. It is absolutely necessary for partners to have sufficient emotional connections so that their bond can remain strong. In the absence of emotional connection, they become resentful of each other and soon the cracks start forming, leading to the falling of the relationship. Space is necessary in a relationship but partners must learn how to strike a balance. They must not go seeking space to the point that their partner wonders whether they are really in a relationship.

- **Despising collaboration**

In a healthy relationship, partners work as a team. They are not scared of working together toward a common goal. However, for a person with insecure attachment issues, they are averse to working as a team, and they prefer working in isolation, because they cannot bring themselves to trust any other person. Usually, they seem to think that no human being is reliable, and for that reason, they can't bring themselves to trust another person enough to work along with them. This attitude invites strain into the relationship because partners need to feel included and the fact that the other person is operating solo can be frustrating.

- **Poor communication**

Another common issue present among people with insecure attachment issues is poor communication. You see, the person has developed an unhealthy mindset toward human beings, and they prefer to just keep things to themselves. But this is an incredibly wrong approach because communication is at the heart of strong relationships. Lack of communication in relationships causes the development of resentment as neither one understands what is really going on with their counterpart, and such a relationship cannot survive for too long before it comes crashing down.

- **Avoiding conflict**

As human beings, we are flawed. When we get into relationships, we don't stop being human beings. From time to time we will create a mess. From time to time we will offend our partner. But it is extremely critical that our partner notices these mistakes and call us out. When you are in a relationship with someone who has insecure attachment issues it appears that they are always avoiding conflict. It's not like they make peace with these issues but they kind of bottle them up. Obviously, these issues will continue piling up, and one day they will burst open, and the relationship will get dismantled.

Preoccupied partners

The preoccupied partner is very anxious. They developed this unhealthy mindset from a young age and they grow up to be unable to form healthy relationships with their partners. These are some of the unhealthy habits of preoccupied partners:

- **Worried about rejection**

Once they get into a relationship, they cannot seem to relax and enjoy what they have. Instead, they are preoccupied with thoughts of what could go wrong. They seem to think that their partner will soon "come to their senses" and get rid of them. these people have dealt with trauma from an early age and they always expect the worst from people. But then being preoccupied with a relationship, wondering all the time what could go wrong, is not the best way to live, and it contributes to conflict because their insecurity will push them into acting in an untoward manner. They have a rigid way of looking at the relationship and even slight deviations could cause them to develop extreme anxiety and worry. Excessive worrying can cause the other person to be resentful which ultimately leads to the deterioration of the relationship.

- **Needy**

Someone who's struggling with insecure attachment issues will tend to act needy. This stems from their need to feel reassured. They cannot sit back and allow their partner to be what they want because they feel threatened. The needy person will force their partner to reassure them over and over again that they still want them. as the relationship advances, the neediness becomes even stronger and this usually causes the other person to become resentful. Obviously, it's nice that your partner wants the reassurance of your love, but then it quickly becomes boring if they are seeking reassurance on the regular and not letting you alone.

- **Ruminate**

This person never has a quiet moment to themselves where they can just relax and enjoy life. Instead, they are preoccupied with immense thoughts about what's going on with their partner. They will carefully consider every little occurrence in the life of their partner and try to assess how it can be a threat to the stability of the relationship. As a result, this contributes to immense anger issues, as the person always seems to have many issues to fight their partner over, and this tendency obviously affects the stability of their relationship in the long run.

- **Unpredictable**

Generally, human beings prefer to get into a relationship with people that they understand. This means that they don't want to be thrown off balance on the regular because of what their partner is doing. But this is what it feels like to be in a relationship with a person with insecure attachment. You can't seem to understand what their next move is going to be and this can be incredibly frustrating. Their partners end up thinking that they have been shortchanged and this usually leads to the demise of the relationship. People want to get involved with someone that they understand totally.

Disorganized partners

This person struggles with insecure attachment issues that are rooted in their unresolved past traumas. They are essentially stuck in their past. In order to overcome their unhealthy mindset, they have to be honest with themselves and confront their past. These are some of the negative habits exhibited by the disorganized partner.

- **Extremely emotional**

As human beings, it's quite okay to feel emotional, depending on what we have been through. But then it reaches a certain point and it becomes just too much. And that's the case with some people that suffer from insecure attachment. They tend to be extremely emotional. They will spend most of their time thinking back to the horrible things that happened to them in their early childhood and grieve about it. This habit denies them the chance to focus on their life and become happy with who they are. It also denies them the chance to become courageous and seek help for their emotional trauma. It seems they would rather get stuck in their past and always think about what was done to them and totally ignore the fact they have the power to overcome their hurt and lead a happy life.

- **Argumentative**

Thanks to their emotional traumas, such a person is always on the prowl for the next fight. It seems they have not only lost trust in fellow human beings but they have become combative against them. it seems they think the world owes them something. Their argumentative nature makes it extremely hard for them to enjoy a positive relationship with other people. They will always find something to grapple about. They will always want to fight about something. They cannot be wrong. And this attitude becomes tiring. Being stuck in a relationship with an argumentative person causes the fast demises of the relationship.

- **Antisocial**

For healthy relationships, people need to develop strong ties with those around them. if they go out, the partners should actively engage in socializing, because it helps stabilize emotions. But for someone who has a past of dealing with untrustworthy human beings, they might have developed an unhealthy mindset that makes it hard for them to socialize with other people freely. Such a person would rather stay indoors than go out and enjoy a night of merry-making. And all of their repressed emotions are usually taken out on their partner through various passive-aggressive means.

- **Cruelty**

They say that hurt people hurt others. If you look at most people who treat people or animals with cruelty, they most likely were hurt in their childhood. This is not an attempt to make an excuse for people who possess immense cruelty, but rather, an admission that such people are likely to have experienced some sort of cruelty themselves. For a person who finds that they are drawn toward hurting other people or animals as a way of settling their emotional issues, they had better seek help, because such a path not only guarantees the end of their relationship, but it sends them on a collision path with the enforcers of law, who couldn't care less about their background.

Chapter 2:

Showing poor attitude & suspicion

The success of a relationship is dependent upon the willingness of the partners to equally put in the effort. When it's only one person that seems to get it right it cannot work, because they eventually become frustrated.

Being in a relationship with someone that struggles with insecure attachment issues can be problematic because they have poor attitude and suspicion; and these two factors are unforgiving agents of ruin. The following are some of the ways that their poor attitude and suspicion comes out.

- **Self-defeating statements**

When a person with insecure attachment issues gets into a relationship, they can easily frustrate their partner with their self-defeating statements. It doesn't matter the potential that this person has, but obviously, they have been conditioned to see themselves in a negative light especially because of the traumatic experiences they underwent in their early childhood. Their partner might know too well that they have potential, and upon urging them to make something of this potential, they will say something along the lines of "I can't!" They are simply trained to sabotage themselves and see themselves as lesser human beings.

- **Negative assumptions**

Another negative tendency of people who are struggling with insecure attachment is negative assumptions. They cannot seem to think on the bright side. When they have to make a decision, they view it in a negative light; when they are faced with a challenge; they view it in a negative light, and this makes it particularly hard for them to make significant progress in life. having negative assumptions not only begets them a foul mood but it always drives people away from them.

- **Comparison with others**

They are not comfortable with who they are. They are always looking to see who's better off or worse off than them. but their eyes are clouded because this comparison comes from a place of self-hate. Constant comparison with others causes them to awaken their insecurities and they have a hard time functioning in society. The fact of the matter is that some people will always be ahead of you, and others will be behind you, but it shouldn't matter, as long as you are working toward your goals. And constantly comparing yourself with others denies you the chance to focus on making yourself a better person.

- **Living in the past**

Let's say that this person grew up in a foster family and their parents weren't particularly loving. Maybe they were beaten up over minor issues. Maybe they were emotionally and verbally abused. But it's far healthier to confront your past and make peace with your past. But then a person who's struggling with insecure attachment issues would rather revisit all the horrible things that happened to them when they were little and vulnerable, and this causes them to be in a state of emotional pain at all times. We cannot undo the past but we can prepare the future by taking our focus off the past and beginning actual work.

- **Victimhood**

Another crippling attitude exhibited by these people is a tendency of viewing themselves as victims. When they are unable to achieve what they were looking to achieve, instead of looking at what they did wrong, they immediately think that the world is against them, that the evil forces are at work. And this mentality of being a victim invites nothing but trouble in their life. being in a relationship with a person with insecure attachment issues means that they will always be looking to get their way lest they accuse you of trying to gain an advantage over them – like people have always done.

- **Blaming others**

It's true that human beings are weak and flawed. But that doesn't mean we should run away from our responsibilities. In a relationship with someone who's battling insecure attachment issues, they will be always looking to pass blame to someone else, and they cannot bring themselves to admit failure. This attitude comes from a place of victimhood and a large ego. They seem to think they are above making any mistakes and it is such a terrible attitude that eventually sabotages a relationship.

- **Unforgiveness**

When two people come into a relationship, obviously they are going to rub each other the wrong way at one time; they are going to err. But then if the erring partner asks for forgiveness it is upon their partner to grant forgiveness. This allows them to bury the hatchet and move on without holding bitter feelings against each other. But then far often people with insecure attachment issues find it hard to forgive. They will hold on to grudges and will never let go until they hurt back the other person.

- **The fear of failure**

Such people tend to stay in their comfort zone. They might be extremely talented and gifted, but they are scared of trying out because they cannot live with the pain of failure. Nothing worth ever accomplishing was easy to do. But they want to swim in the familiar waters, because they are assured of stability. But then this is a great disservice to both themselves and their partner. If only they had tried to leave their comfort zone, they would have attained significant success that would have helped them address their deep-rooted issues.

- **Criticism**

Another way that people battling insecure attachment seem to act is through their excessive criticism. They seem to have a sharp eye for details and no matter what their partner has done, they will always come at them with criticism. It stems from their unhealthy attitude toward human beings developed in their childhood. And it also comes from a place of wanting to hit back at human beings so they can feel good about themselves. Sadly, criticism does more harm than good to a relationship, as it causes their partner to feel resentful.

- **Contempt**

One of the major factors behind the high divorce rates in America is contempt. When we talk of contempt, we are talking of your significant other staring you down as though you are a dirty flea, calling out nasty insults because they have no respect for you, and a multitude of other nasty things. It is a common characteristic among people who struggle with insecure attachment issues. They seem to hold their partners in contempt. They simply have no respect. And this tendency causes their partners to become discouraged. In the end, it brings about the ruin of the relationship.

- **Mind games**

Also, the person who's struggling with insecure attachment issues is not mature enough to engage their partners in order to overcome a conflict, instead they are looking for dominance through mind games. They never tire of it. Of course, repeated mind games only make the situation worse, and their partner becomes more resentful, and one day they cannot take it anymore, bringing the relationship to an end. The mind games can be centered around trivial things that aren't supposed to bother a well-adjusted couple. Apart from being tiring, mind games also denote tremendous disrespect.

- **Lecturing**

The person struggling with insecure attachment issues may take on the role of a nasty parent so that they lecture their partner over every minor thing. Of course, no adult would take such an attitude lightly. Once they see their partner lecturing them more than once, it occurs to them that their partner has lost their respect, and from here things can only go worse. This tendency of lecturing partners comes from a place of believing that they are better than everybody else, and thus, much better poised to dictate how things should go.

Apart from a poor attitude, the partner struggling with insecure attachment issues will also commonly demonstrate suspicion, and this can quickly send the relationship on the rocks. The common factors of suspicion in a relationship are as follows:

- **Doubt**

When doubt seeps into the relationship, the affected partner will notice that their actions are more scrutinized, and they cannot be left alone to do as they please. Their partner seems to follow them around, asking more questions than is normal, all in an attempt to find inconsistencies. The insecure person cannot bring himself to trust the actions of their counterpart and so they have to check them constantly, but such a habit causes the other person to become uncomfortable because they would expect that their partner believed in them. in a relationship, people shouldn't work like rivals, but they should work as a team, thus there must be trust and openness, but doubt extinguishes all of that.

- **Distrust**

After a doubt finds its way into the relationship, then it is escalated into distrust. One of the common things that people fight over is money. Let's say the insecure partner starts to doubt how their partner is handling their income. Maybe he thinks that she is not handling money as she should. He will keep following her around, asking leading questions, trying to find out whether or not she is engaging in unfair practices, desperate to latch on a thread of accusation. At this point, he cannot bring himself to trust her with money again, and so he will start declining cooperation, and making it hard for her to access the couple's income, because he believes that she's driven by selfishness, even though there's no evidence to support the belief. Normally, their finances should go to hell, but more than that, the distrust spreads to all other parts of their relationship. They start having problems in the kitchen, in the bedroom, in the bathroom, and before long the relationship is getting licked by the tongues of conflict.

- **Anxiety**

Now that there's sufficient tension between the partners, this leads to the emergence of anxiety. Both of them are stuck with terrible thoughts, imagining what could go wrong, guessing how their partner could act, and this sends them into a grip of immense anxiety. Once people are struggling with anxiety, it becomes hard for them to be productive, because they are distracted by negative thoughts as to what the other person might be up to.

Eventually, anxiety causes the partners to become hostile to one another. If the whole problem stemmed from finance issues, it means that they will soon start sabotaging each other's efforts to get access to the money, and such hostility, given time, culminates in untold viciousness. Anxiety also tends to make it hard for people to reason their decisions through, and you find that the relationship takes a dive into the bottomless pit of failed relationships, as the partners jump from one nasty decision to another even nastier, and before long, the relationship is dead.

- **Fear**

Have you ever heard of a couple whereby one of them is so distrustful that they take a weapon to the bed? It's crazy that people who once swore to being unable to live without the other could take their relationship to such high hostility. But this is what happens after the seeds of doubt have given birth to distrust and anxiety. They cannot bring themselves to bring each other. They each think that the other is out to get them. And this makes it particularly hard to develop a harmonious relationship. A person with insecure attachment issues is likely to be engulfed in fear because their self-preservation instinct is loudest considering they have gone through pain before – in their traumatic earlier years.

18

- **Fighting**

All of the distrust culminates into a fight. The partner with insecure attachment issues cannot take any more. They are usually the aggressor. Of course, the length of the fight depends on the kind of opponent they have. If it's the un-surrendering partner, then war is on, but if it's the harmonious partner, there's a quick ceasefire and things come back to normal. A relationship can still be salvaged after fighting but the relationship hardly ever goes back to what it once had been.

Chapter 3:

Constant anxiety & depression

Anxiety is a pretty normal biological force that has enabled us to survive the hostile environments of the ancient ages. When we are feeling anxious, perhaps the mind is calling us to attention over a serious matter, trying to save us.

But then again there's nothing great about having anxiety basically all the time, but this is the reality of most people who have insecure attachment issues.

Such people tend to sabotage their relationship thanks to their uncontrollable anxiety and depression. The following are some of the ways that anxiety contributes to ruining a relationship.

- **Clinginess**

A person with insecure attachment issues is bound to have negative beliefs, and these negative beliefs form a web and slowly expand, overwhelming the individual. The person might start thinking that they are going to lose their partner – an unbearable thought. And this causes them to start clinging on their partner, under the misguided impression that clinging on them will stop them from leaving their partner. More often than not, the clingy person ends up getting what he most feared, for when he clings onto their partner, this brings about resentment, and the partner becomes determined to escape the claws of their clingy partner. Also, being clingy erodes their respect, because there's an instant power shift in favor of their partner, who is free to do as they please, or else the partner threatens to leave.

- **Possessiveness**

The person with insecure attachment issues will also ruin their relationship through their tendency of acting as though they own their partner. Basically, it's clinginess taken a step further. By acting possessive, this person tries to control everything that their partner is doing. It never occurs to them that their partner is busy with their life and expects privacy. But the possessive person will indulge in all manner of activities in a bid to control their partner. Of course, this causes their partner to become resentful, and they begin to fight back, looking for a way to make a clean escape from this toxic person. Being possessive of another person is akin to asking for heartbreak because you force your target to fight for independence. But then the possessive person rarely looks at it that way. They are just desperate to see that they can control their target in a bid to discourage them from running away.

- **Jealousy**

Also, the person with insecure attachment issues will develop jealousy toward their partner. The need to be possessive of their partner stems from their obsession with being able to control them but they are also looking to spy on what is going on in their partner's life. For instance, they may take their social media logins, and start snooping through their feeds, checking to see what kind of material their partner is consuming, what kind of people their partner is keeping in contact with. If it appears that their partner is having a great life, the person will become jealous, and try to look for ways to sabotage their partner's happiness.

- **Isolation**

In some cases, people with insecure attachment issues decide to go all out and act dramatic as they try to domesticate their partner. But in some other cases, anxiety causes the person to become docile. They withdraw from society. But this withdrawal is also driven by low self-esteem. Isolation can be a dangerous thing because it denies you a chance to interact with other human beings and it denies you access to resources. This tendency to isolate oneself doesn't help the relationship; instead it drives the partner into seeking contact elsewhere, effectively ruining what they once had.

- **Poor communication**

Another way that anxiety shows itself is through closed communication channels. Generally, for a relationship to become stable, partners need to engage with each other pretty openly. But the person with insecure attachment issues will be driven into exhibiting poor communication habits thanks to their anxiety. One of the common things that such people do is stonewalling. They sabotage any attempt by their partner to have a productive conversation by delaying the conversation or flat out refusing to participate. Poor communication eventually causes the frustrated party to become extremely resentful, sending the relationship onto the rocks.

- **Viciousness**

In a relationship, people should be happy and comfortable around their partners. But then when you are dealing with someone with insecure attachment issues, expect some viciousness. The insecure person has probably lived through many nasty experiences and it has put in him a fighting spirit. And thus, any slight, whether real or imagined, is to be met with viciousness. The problem with being vicious in a relationship is that it triggers fighting. And once partners begin to fight then the only thing ahead is doom.

- **Procrastination**

Once anxiety sets in, it causes people to have a terribly negative mindset, and causes them to develop negative beliefs. When a person is struggling with negative beliefs, they are unlikely to be productive, because this shatters their self-belief. As a result, such a person tends to procrastinate even more. Obviously, procrastination is a bad habit and causes people to lead unfulfilled lives. The more a person procrastinates, the more they deny themselves a chance to become a better person, and this usually ends with them being resentful, and misguidedly fighting anyone around them, particularly their partners.

- **Selfishness**

In a relationship, people should act like a team. This means that you shouldn't hold on too much to what you own and forget to share with the other person. You should be willing to share your resources with your partner. But then for a person with insecure attachment issues, sharing is a foreign term, and they are only inclined to use the other person. They like being selfish. And this causes their relationship to experience a lot of difficulties. But funny enough, they expect their partner to be generous with their resources, and if this expectation is not met, there is hell to pay.

- **Anger issues**

Another way anxiety brings out its ugly head is through the immense anger issues. An anxious person tends to be negative most of the time. They are always thinking too hard and always imagining that things are getting out of hand. And this tendency causes them to develop major anger issues. Being in a relationship with such a person can be somewhat tricky because they are going to go off on you many times. Anger issues only tend to make things worse.

- **Taking things personally**

Also, anxiety tends to drive such people into always taking things personally. They almost don't have a well-adjusted way of looking at life. but they seem to be taking everything that you tell them personally. And obviously this habit leads them to develop friction with a lot of people in their life. The fact is that no one can have full control of what happens in their life. But in order to survive through the various life challenges we go through, we should have a good attitude, but this is foreign to most people who are battling various forms of anxiety, and they end up crushing their relationship.

A person with insecurity attachment issues tends to also struggle with depression. When you are in the grip of depression, most things stop making sense and also you tend to lose hope. Some of the ways that depression ruins relationships include:

- **Low spirits**

When a person is depressed, you are likely to hear that they feel "low". But this feeling isn't just emotional but physical too. They feel as though they have no energy and cannot cope with normal life activities. When you are in a relationship there are various things that you are expected to be doing, and all of these activities take energy. However, when you are low, you cannot partake of these activities because you are in a bad place both emotionally and physically. Being in perpetually low spirits tends to make life unbearable and causes people to experience problems in their relationships.

- **Withdrawal**

Depression is a pretty common feeling however when it is persistent, it ruins everything. Depression causes people to become withdrawn from their partners. The person with insecure attachment issues is bound to be nursing some form of depression because of the nasty experiences they lived through in their childhood. As a result, they might develop hard feelings against their spouse, and cause them to stay away from their spouse. Depression tends to take away the pleasure from everything and leaves you fighting for sanity. The more a person is depressed, the more likely they are to withdraw from their partners, because they feel that they are not deserving of happiness. In order to overcome depression, one must admit that they need help, and they must be willing to receive help. However, most people who are depressed tend to indulge in self-deceit and this makes the situation even far worse.

- **Impatience**

Many of us seem impatient with other people. And this is especially true in this era of technological advancement. But for someone who's struggling with insecure attachment issues, the impatience is on another level; it borders on madness. In worst-case scenario, you will be left that something is wrong with you, or that you are insane, because your partner is hellbent on driving you insane. If they ask for something, you had better avail right then, or they will think that you are sabotaging their plans. These impatient people have a flawed way of perceiving life and they can twist almost any circumstance in order to make it seem you are in their way.

- **Low sex drive**

Let's face it, intimacy, and particularly sexual intimacy, is necessary in a relationship. But then most depressed people are preoccupied with their problems, and they cannot get themselves to think about having a nice romantic time with their partner. Depression causes them to have a low sex drive. And this causes the person to start evading their partner; if they are touched, they recoil like a rat, and they always make excuses to stay away from their partner. Of course, such behavior is deeply frustrating on their partner, and this leads to tremendous problems in the relationship.

- **Dim outlook**

The depressed person can hardly see the greatness in their life or their partner's life. This is because they have a negative outlook on most things. The depression makes it hard for them to become well-adjusted and enjoy life. The pain that they endured in their childhood triggers this depression and makes it hard for them to have a bright outlook on life. This dim outlook spills into most other areas and causes the person to behave like a robot. It is totally unbecoming to always have a negative outlook on life.

- **Development of addictions**

When we talk of addictions, most people seem to think about drugs and alcohol. But in as much as people are commonly addicted to drugs and alcohol, there are other forms of addiction that are not as obvious. For a person who' struggling with insecure attachment issues, they will always find themselves developing various addictions including food addiction, sex addiction, video game addiction, and work addiction. The purpose of addiction is that it provides an escape from the nasty reality. But then these people forget that you can only run from your problems for so long.

- **Self-doubt**

The world can be a very ruthless stage. There are enough things trying to bring us down, make us think less of ourselves. Depression causes one to think that they are not good enough. And this causes them to start exhibiting self-inhibiting habits. In order to achieve success, you not only need skills and talent, but you also need to believe that you are capable of achieving success, or else you'll be cast aside when the going gets tough, as it always does. But people who are depressed always seem to have doubts about their potential and this stops them from being happy and also tarnishes the quality of their relationship.

Chapter 4:

Endless drama & obsessive disorder

Every relationship has its fair share of drama. Actually, it can be argued that some level of drama is necessary to keep the relationship tight. However, the problem comes in when you are stuck with a partner who's dramatic all the time. And this is the case with most people who are suffering from insecurity attachment issues. They are always looking to do something because they feel threatened about their position in that relationship. The following are some of the common ways that people with insecure attachment issues display their dramatic side.

- **Yelling**

When you have an issue, they don't know how to handle it with decorum, and they make sure to make the scene dramatic. They yell. They are looking for attention. They are looking to get their partner shocked into submission. Not only is this behavior embarrassing but it also points to their lack of respect. The person with insecure attachment issues comes from a place of having endured too much in their life and this behavior is a misguided effort to show they are unwilling to take any more hurt.

- **Cheating**

Their dramatic side comes out too through their cheating habits. A person with insecure attachment issues might go out looking for a cheating partner and not even think too much of it, and actually attempt to justify their actions, saying that the other person cheats as well. They are emotionally damaged in that they think no one can be trusted and all humans are out to satisfy their selfish needs. They forget to realize that in a relationship, people must guard their carnal desires, and avoid cheating so as to keep the relationship intact. They engage in such habits because they are looking for some drama.

- **Lying**

A person struggling with insecure attachment issues will have a tendency of telling lies. It's a thing for them. They cannot help it. They even tell lies when there's no need to. It comes from a place of wanting to avoid pain. They have been conditioned to think that truth hurts and therefore they had better craft a lie and believe in it. Of course, such mentality is toxic, and in the long run, it brings them tremendous pain. Lying not only ruins a relationship but it also antagonizes the world around and causes you to be despised.

- **Selfishness**

A person with insecure attachment issues can be driven into acting selfish because they think that only their needs matter. They have no respect for the feelings and needs of other people. It also stems from a place of wanting to preserve themselves because they have a skewed perception of human beings. They think of human beings are predators who must be shunned. And this causes them to be selfish about their resources. This attitude undermines the resourcefulness of a relationship considering that a relationship requires two people to contribute toward each other's happiness.

- **Violence**

Some people are very daring. When they have an issue with you, yelling and calling you names won't be enough, but they have to lunge at you, grab you by the neck, and hit at you. Such people usually have severe attachment issues and their violence especially comes in when there is a problem that threatens the security of that relationship. Also, it might be that they were physically assaulted in their childhood, and they, in turn, became very sensitive, so much so the only way they can answer any dispute is through violence.

- **Stonewalling their spouse**

No two people on this earth are in a relationship devoid of dispute. We are human beings. Whether we like it or not, we must make mistakes, and we rely on the forgiveness of our partners in order to move along. But there are people who don't believe in working through a problem; they had much rather delay the process and make the situation worse. When a conflict comes up, instead of engaging their partner, and finding out what the problem really was, they shun their partner and refuse to engage, making the situation dimmer.

- **Crying**

Well, crying is a very normal thing. We should cry when we are hurt. We should cry when we are overjoyed. But people with insecure attachment issues cry for different reasons altogether; to get their way. Say, you are in the middle of an argument, and it seems you are holding your ground; the insecure person throws their mouth open and starts crying, hoping to gain your sympathy and make you accept what they want. Such a habit is terribly manipulative. In the long run, their partner is disillusioned and they want out.

- **Weaponizing sex**

Another terrible thing that people with insecure attachment issues do is using sex as a weapon. If they want something that their partner is not willing or able to give, then they deny their partner sex until their partner gives in to their demand. This is a vicious move. We all know that sex plays a great role in the unity of a relationship. In the absence of a strong sex life, the relationship just falls apart. When one partner weaponizes sex, they make the other person bitter and resentful. Weaponizing sex can also terribly backfire when you are dealing with someone with tremendous sexual discipline or someone who doesn't really care.

- **Erratic behavior**

This involves going out of your way to cause a scene in order to settle a perceived wrong. This is especially common amongst women. Maybe she caught him with another woman, and instead of letting the man explain, or instead of resolving the issue behind closed doors, she quickly started defacing his car or burning his clothes. Not only is erratic behavior deeply inconveniencing but it can also throw one on a collision path with the law. It doesn't matter what the other person has done, it's always best to have a conversation instead of going rogue.

- **Messy**

When someone has gotten into a relationship, they are old enough to make proper decisions, and take care of themselves. It is common to see the person with insecure attachment issues acting messy. It stems from their childhood, for they may not have someone to check over them, instruct them on the right way of living, and now they are stuck with behaving as they wish. It's not okay to expect that your partner will clean up after you or baby you. Being in a relationship you are adult enough to take care of yourself.

- **Gossip**

Insecure attachment might cause people to become extreme gossipers. There's nothing wrong with a little bit of gossip about something you both share an interest. However, if someone is indulging in gossip for the sake of it, if every waking minute is spent in dispensing some gossip, there's a huge problem. This tendency of people with insecure attachment issues to gossip comes from a place of comparing themselves with other people. They always feel compelled to gossip so that they can make themselves feel better. But this is obviously not a sustainable way of improving themselves because in order to feel great about yourself you must address your deep-seated issues.

The person battling insecure attachment issues might also exhibit various habits that indicate an obsessive disorder. Some of these habits include:

- **Contacting the other person excessively**

In a relationship with an insecure person, they will always be looking to establish contact, wanting to find out where you are, what you are doing, whom you are hanging out with. They cannot be satisfied to know that you are out there making your own decisions. When you are at home, they will be around you, winning your attention, and when you step out, they keep contact through texts, and emails, and phone calls, but it's not like they are looking to have a meaningful discussion, except it's their latest effort to monitor you. Of course, their partner will frown upon such behavior and express disgust over being followed around like that.

- **Constant need for reassurance**

The person with insecure attachment disorder will always be looking to be reassured that they are still an item. They are scared of the idea that the relationship could fall apart. And in order to feel secure again, they have to ask their partner to reassure them that everything is all right. It gets old. This habit seems to achieve the opposite of what they wished. Instead of making their partner happier, they instead drive them away, so that the partner begins to look for a way to evade this person. Strong relationships require people who give each other space. Strong relationships require people to be happy about who they are; they have to be self-assured, but when one starts to behave as though they cannot do without the other, it causes the other one to be uncomfortable, and they might want out.

- **Deserting friends**

Friends play a critical role in our lives. Many studies show that people who have friends lead happier lives. Just because you are in a relationship, it doesn't mean that you won't need to have any friends around you. You will always need friends. Codependent relationships are not as healthy as one might imagine. For people with insecure attachment disorders, it is not uncommon for them to desert their friends, so that they may spend more time with their partner. This is a terrible move on their part. They fail to acknowledge the fact that things might go south down the road but their friends would help them get over their grief. And once you don't have any friend by your side, then should things go haywire then you are in for a nasty ride.

- **Burying their needs**

As human beings, we are not like, but that's the beauty of life. It would actually be terrible if we were all alike. For a person with insecure attachment issues, they will always suppress their needs, and embrace the lifestyle of their partner. This is akin to giving up their happiness and it's uncalled for. Stable relationships require partners to have their own lives so that they can have a way of recharging. People with attachment issues suppress their needs and ape their partner because they are looking for acceptance. It comes from a place of being unhappy with who they are. Maybe they have gone through tremendous pain and they have always thought that something was wrong with them. They hope that by shunning their needs and embracing the activities of their partner they will be liked more, but that's not usually the case. In actual fact, such a habit is likely to repel their partner.

- **Protecting their partner**

It might seem ludicrous, but the person with insecure attachment issues will commonly tr to protect their partner. They can't seem to let their partner handle their problems like the adult they are. Instead, they will always butt in, rushing to defend their partner. In a relationship it is necessary for both partners to have each other's back, however, it is not okay for one person to keep jumping into every situation that their partner gets involved in, trying to defend them. They need to let their counterpart lead their life without feeling the need to intrude over trivial issues.

- **Low self-esteem**

People who obsess about their partner tend to have low self-esteem. This low self-esteem stops them from leading a normal life and so they make it all about their significant other. Relationships are not the end all be all. People should have a life outside of their relationship. But a person struggling with insecure attachment issues is likely to have low self-esteem that stops them from leading a quality life. low self-esteem also causes them to lose themselves and let their partner call the shots, which is not a good thing in a relationship, because both partners need to be heard.

Chapter 5:

Irresponsible behavior

For a relationship to stand the test of time, both partners must take responsibility. They must be willing to take care of the relationship and ensure that everything is smooth-sailing. For a person with insecure attachment issues, they are likely to exhibit various irresponsible habits, and this usually invites problems into the relationship. Some of the habits that denote irresponsibility include:

- **Ridicule**

This is the tendency of one or both partners to put each other down. Such a habit can only harm the relationship. For the success of a relationship, partners should have immense love for one another, and it should never occur to them that it is okay to put each other down. In most cases, it starts innocently enough, but within a short moment, the partners start really going at each other. It is never okay to ridicule each other because it makes one or both partners embarrassed. And knowing that human beings have an ego, it can drive the offended party int striking back, effectively starting a war that could very well take down the entire relationship. But when you decide to respect each other nothing terrible goes down.

- **Withholding information**

Another habit that demonstrates irresponsible behavior is a tendency to withhold information. In a relationship, both partners should trust each other. When one or both partners start withholding information from each other it means that the trust is gone and they need to work on bringing it back. Withholding crucial information might push someone into making the wrong decision. People with insecure attachment issues have been brought up to expect the worst from other human beings. And this is precisely what causes them to withhold crucial information and keep their partner in the dark.

- **Emotional distance**

Most people who keep emotional distance are commonly manipulative. They are hoping to bring their partner to the knees so that they can get their way. People with insecure attachment issues might develop this habit because they are misguidedly preserving themselves from pain. Considering that emotional intimacy is necessary in a strong relationship, by being emotionally distant, you only make your partner bitter. And they might decide to call it a day and look for someone else who is not going to play games with them. being emotionally distant indicates that you are not interested in keeping the relationship anyway.

- **Disengagement**

This is generally preceded by loss of emotional intimacy. At this point, one or both partners seem to have little patience for each other, or in other words, they couldn't care less. If something is not done, the relationship will fall into pieces pretty soon. When one or both partners have stopped caring it means they have no hope for the relationship. It means they are at their wits end on how to keep the relationship alive. A person with insecure attachment issues first tries with their might to corner their partner, but once it proves futile, they disengage and wait for the worst.

- **Passive-aggressiveness**

Being passive-aggressive means that you have a hard time being upfront and cooperating with other people. It is just as bad to be aggressive; whereby you act forceful about your needs. It is far more beneficial to be assertive. Being assertive means that one is not afraid to express their needs and wishes in an eloquent manner. Assertive behavior is what causes you to earn respect. Some people with insecure attachment issues might lack the courage to be assertive, and they resort to resisting their partners indirectly, and this invites problems into the relationship.

- **Unforgiveness**

In a relationship, it is the responsibility of partners to forgive one another. As human beings, we will always be at fault, but then we depend on the willingness of our partners to forgive. When partners begin to act with hostility and viciousness toward each other, it means that they have lost respect for each other, and also, they are not willing to make their relationship strong. When one or both partners cannot bring themselves to forgive, it causes the relationship to fall apart, and this hostility drives them into becoming sworn enemies.

- **Spreading rumors**

Love is a powerful force. If love is denied a chance to blossom, it might very easily turn into hatred. One of the ways that hatred is manifest between lovers is through spreading of rumors. It usually takes place after one or both partners are hurt. They spread rumors in an attempt to get even. But it is a reckless move that is likely to cause the demise of the relationship. Words are powerful. When you assassinate someone's character, they cannot possibly have their former life back, for people are superficial, and they will keep talking ill, even though the rumors are dispelled.

- **Addiction**

Another habit that denotes irresponsibility is addiction. Life is tough. Relationships are hard work. There is no easy way out. You must be willing to take the long and hard road. But then most people are weak and they want to escape reality. Thus, they resort to all forms of addictions. By turning to drugs and alcohol it shows that you have given up hope and that you are willing to ruin your relationship so that you might carry on with your vices. People with insecure attachment issues are likely to resort to drugs and alcohol because they don't have the emotional strength to handle reality.

- **Verbal abuse**

Verbal abuse brings about shame, embarrassment, and pain. People who resort to verbal abuse clearly have no respect for their partners. When in a relationship, you should do your best to protect your partner from shame and embarrassment, and this means you must not verbally abuse them in public. Granted, your partner might have done something really nasty, but even then, they deserve to be chastised in privacy, where it's only between you. People with insecure attachment issues are likely to go off on their partner when they feel slighted.

- **Physical abuse**

Worse than verbal abuse. When you take the extra step of assaulting your partner because of your differences, you have got it totally wrong. Physical abuse not only embarrasses the victim but it could very well jeopardize their health. Also, when a relationship reaches the stage where partners must exchange blows to make a point, it shows that they have become totally irresponsible. Some people with insecure attachment issues might have been physically abused during their childhood and once they come of age they take to violence. But then such behavior is irresponsible and causes tremendous hurt in the long run.

- **Loss of respect**

People with insecure attachment issues can have a hard time staying in love with someone. It reaches a point and the conflict becomes too much and it feels like it was better to call it quits and move on to something else. At this point, the respect is lost. This means that they stop giving their partner's values and needs any importance. They start viewing their partner as though they never mattered. And this attitude guarantees that their relationship tumbles down. For any relationship to become stable, partners must have respect for one another.

- **No physical intimacy**

Physical intimacy is as important as emotional intimacy for the survival of a relationship. But what happens when partners are having a hard time, you will find one partner becoming more disinterested in physical intimacy than the other. Obviously, this is a bad move if they intend to keep the relationship. A human being's mating instinct is powerful. Nothing would incite more resentment than being paired with a partner who resists physical intimacy. It makes one resentful. A person with insecure attachment issues is likely to develop an aversion to physical intimacy when they feel overwhelmed by life and this could cause their partner to become bitter about it.

- **Dishonesty**

Another behavior that sabotages a relationship is dishonesty. It's one thing to withhold information and it's entirely another thing to mislead your partner. Yet, many people indulge in dishonest practices, aimed at fooling their partners. Being dishonest means that you have no respect whatsoever for your partner and you wouldn't even care what misery befalls them. Once the other party finds out that they were misled, they develop tremendous resentment, and it kills any chances of ever having a stable relationship. People with insecure attachment issues tend to become dishonest in a misguided attempt to self-preserve considering that they have a flawed perception of humanity.

- **Jealousy**

Lovers could hold tremendous jealousy against each other. But in such a case, their love is suffocated, and it becomes hard for them to have a stable relationship. A person with insecure attachment issues might have been brought up to think himself inadequate. And so, he might be looking around, comparing himself with other people, and always seeing what they have and he doesn't. This mindset obviously causes him to become jealous of their partner, and virtually anyone else that he considers to have an advantage over him. Such a way of living is not only harmful but pitiful as well. It doesn't matter how strong their partner's love had been, but the jealous on him just can't let them have a stable relationship.

- **Sexually focused**

It's one thing to have physical intimacy and it's entirely another thing to be primarily focused on sex. When a relationship is driven primarily by sex, there's not a strong emotional connection to stabilize the relationship, and this could cause the relationship to fall apart. Also, it is necessary to strike a balance, for overindulgence in sex might cause the partners to eventually become bored with it, and this could lead to severe cracks in the relationship.

- **Narcissism**

Narcissism never goes well with relationships. A narcissistic individual is manipulative and ruthless and they will stop at nothing as they advance to gain what they want. People with insecure attachment issues are more likely to exhibit narcissistic tendencies because of their troubled childhood. They believe that by manipulating other people they will be protecting themselves against being taken advantage of. But then narcissism tends to make their partners resentful and soon the relationship just falls apart.

- **Misuse of resources**

In this world, resources are limited. We cannot afford to misuse them. One of the main factors that cause high divorce rates in America is disagreement over money. So, one of the irresponsible behaviors that ultimately lead to the demise of a relationship is a tendency to misuse resources. This habit can be observed amongst people with insecure attachment issues. It comes from a place of wanting to fit in. For instance, if someone for the longest time believed that they were not worthy, always thought that they were unwanted, once they have access to some funds, they will start to spend resources in a reckless manner just so they might win people's approval.

- **Competitiveness**

In a relationship, you are not competitors, but rather you are a team. It is totally wrong for relationship partners to become competitive because it shows they lack the meaning of being in a relationship. People with insecure attachment issues are more likely to compete against their partners because they have a deep hole inside of them that they want to cover. They feel that by competing against their partners, they can manage to finally cover this hole, but this is not always the case. One may not overcome their issues by looking to the outside. It is only through confronting their deep-seated issues that one may overcome their troubles.

- **Threats**

Another terrible habit that people have is a tendency to threaten their pattern hoping that it will straighten them. This often backfires. People have an ego. It doesn't matter that you are not a big fan of their actions. But then there's a far better way of getting a partner to change their way as opposed to making threats. People with insecure attachment issues might demonstrate a propensity to threaten their partners because they are always looking to acquire more power for themselves and become bigger.

Part II: Causes

Chapter 6:

Childhood trauma

The experiences that we have as children can play a critical role in how we turn out. If we had a terrible childhood, we are likely to grow up maladjusted. For most people with insecure attachment issues, childhood abuse is one of the major causes. Children are extremely vulnerable and the emotional or physical hurt that they experience comes to haunt them much later. The following are some of the experiences that can be traumatic for children.

- **Domestic violence**

In some dysfunctional homes, parents can be cruel. It normally starts with them going for each other, but soon enough they start focusing on their kids. Kids who have been physically abused tend to endure a lot of trauma, and once they become young adults, they exhibit various issues including insecure attachment. Domestic violence leaves the kid forever scarred as they remember the pain they endured at the hands of their parent or guardian. Also, domestic violence can stem from their siblings or any other person around them. Kids who have faced domestic violence might also grow up to be cruel and violent themselves or they might become extremely fragile.

- **Abandonment**

Kids are vulnerable. They need to grow up in the warmth of loving parents. But some kids are unfortunate in the sense that they have parents who couldn't care less. Their parents might be emotionally distant or have a tendency of leaving them for long periods. It never turns out well. Kids need to have both parents around so that they can become emotionally stable. For kids who are struggling with abandonment issues, it becomes increasingly hard for them to adjust to society, and it gives rise to a number of mental health issues.

- **Sexual abuse**

It is probably one of the worst things that a kid could have to endure. Kids who are sexually abused tend to have a hard time fitting in society. This is because sexual violence tends to destroy a person's emotional stability. The trauma that comes about as a result of sexual abuse is unrivaled. It is life-long too. The person might seek help and all of that but still they will feel haunted by memories of what happened to them. subjecting a kid to sexual abuse is quite simply ruining their life.

- **Verbal abuse**

Another experience that sends a kid into trauma is verbal abuse. This usually happens when one or both of their parents are mentally unstable. In most cases, the verbally abusive parent tends to come from a place of being hurt themselves. But then again two wrongs don't make a right. It doesn't matter that they were hurt too, but they should have the sense to stop the cycle of hurt, and start treating their kids with more respect. Verbal abuse makes a kid deeply resentful. It affects their self-esteem and causes them to have a hard time fitting in society. They also develop insecure attachment issues.

- **Loss of a loved one**

At the end of the day, we are just mortals. We inevitably have to leave this planet. But the problem is that some people leave the planet whilst having dependents. When a kid loses their loved one, particularly their parent, they can have a hard time adjusting in society, because they no longer have the necessary emotional stability. Loss of a loved one can cause a kid to have a terrible attitude too, because they have the wrong impression of the world; they think that the world is out to get them, they think that nothing goes on in the world, and it can send them on the wrong path.

- **Accidents**

Another experience that could send a kid into trauma is an accident. The more technologically advanced we are, the more machines we have to operate, and the more risk we subject ourselves to. If a kid is involved in an accident, for instance, road accident, they could be scarred for life, because they have no conception of how to process the events. It might cause them to develop a negative attitude toward life because they are afraid of the next tragedy.

- **Life-threatening illnesses**

Thank heavens we are at a stage when we have eliminated most medical problems from the planet. But then there are far many illnesses still left, and some even terrible illnesses keep coming up. A kid who is battling some form of illness is in a world of pain and they can be left traumatized for the rest of their life. Kids are very aware of what's going on. Being ill stops them from being a normal kid. It gets in the way of their fun. It causes them to have a negative outlook on life.

- **Natural disasters**

As we continue to burden mother earth with our mindless activities, mother earth will find ways of striking back, and you better be sure that when mother earth strikes back, there's a large trail of destruction. One of the common ways that mother earth strikes back is through hurricanes. It hits the coastal cities and brings the buildings down. Kids who witness that are left traumatized for the rest of their life. Various emotional issues, including insecure attachment issues, can stem from such a traumatic experience.

- **Refugee experience**

Again, the world is in relative political stability, but still there are people in certain corners of the world who are still fighting. Kids who are native to such places and have to be carried away as refugees have a hard time developing emotional stability. Refugee camps cannot provide the warmth that a kid is entitled to.

- **Bullying**

Kids are sweet, but they can also be nasty, especially against their fellow kids. Bullying starts in the early schooling years and could last until high school. But it leaves the target devastated. Kids who have been bullied could have a hard time fitting in and developing the emotional stability necessary to become self-sufficient. They could develop insecure attachment issues that would make it difficult for them to have normal relationships.

It is extremely important for parents to watch their kids so that they might be able to spot when something is amiss. When a kid is going through trauma, it is not always apparent, and this frustrates them even more, because no help is forthcoming, and they cannot really frame what they are experiencing.

These are some of the responses and behavioral changes in children that might be indicative of a traumatic experience.

- **Fear**

When a child is going through a traumatic experience, the first expression they have is fear. They exhibit signs of terror as they feel threatened. For instance, if a child is undergoing bullying at school, they might not always disclose it, because they are embarrassed about what they are going through, but they will always appear scared for their life. You can spot the fear in their eyes, in their hesitation, and they will be extra careful about what they say or do. These are clear signs that the child is going through a traumatic experience. It is important for the parent or guardian to take notice of what's happening.

- **Anxiety**

Anxiety starts pretty early. When a child is experiencing anxiety, it is usually as a result of the traumatic experience that they are going through. For instance, if a kid has just lost their parent, they look around and see that their momma or dad is not around anymore, and they just feel anxious. Nothing ever feels the same anymore. They are looking for ways to express their pain but they can't even conceptualize it. Their anxiety stops them from becoming well-adjusted. It stops them from being happy. They cannot fit in among other kids. And this is painful.

- **Depression**

Also, kids can be depressed. It usually occurs when a kid is going through a traumatic experience. They don't have the emotional stability to process their feelings and make sense of what is happening in their life, and so, they shut off. Most kids who are depressed have a tendency of hiding themselves. They don' want to spend time with their friends or their family, and they are always keeping to themselves. And this makes it hard for them to have an easy time. Depressed kids will also have antisocial tendencies, and in the quiet of their room, they might weep.

- **Nightmares**

Dreams are a way for our subconscious to make sense of various things in our life. kids who are going through a traumatic time of it will experience nightmares on the regular. These nightmares will keep them awake because they are in the middle of making sense of what is happening to them. If you notice that a kid is struggling with nightmares, it might be an indication that they are going through a traumatic experience. Also, it is not a good sign when a kid has difficulties falling asleep; it means that they too are having traumas.

- **Loss of appetite**

Considering that kids are growing up, they require a lot of energy, and this is made clear through their massive eating. So, it's a bad sign when a kid is not eating enough. It indicates that the kid is going through a traumatic experience. For instance, when a kid runs into bullies at school and keeps quiet about it, you might notice them first withdrawing, and then they will begin to lose appetite. Kids are supposed to have an appetite because their body needs more nutrition. Thus, it might be a sign of trauma when a kid won't indulge in food with enthusiasm.

- **Trouble forming relationships**

Another clear sign that a child is going through trauma is an inability to form relationships with other people. This inability to form relationships with other people is usually driven by their anxiety and fears. Relationships play an important role in our lives and failure to form meaningful relationships is also a bad sign. The kid is against forming any relationships with other people because they have developed the wrong outlook on life; they think that human beings are not to be trusted, that human beings only bring trouble, and therefore human beings need to be shunned.

- **Inability to trust anyone**

When a kid experiences trauma at the hands of an individual, especially their parent, they will come away thinking that human beings at large mean them harm, and they will make a point of avoiding every last human being, or at least not trust them ever again. And this is one of the reasons why it's hard for them to have any meaningful relationship with other people. A kid who has deep trust issues tends to be a loner, because only then they are in charge of the whole process, and they can rely on themselves.

- **Difficulty concentrating**

Another indicator that a kid is going through a traumatic experience is an inability to concentrate. They tend to have a faraway look, because they are lost thinking about the trauma they are having, and it is quite hard for them to overcome this pain.

- **Poor academic performance**

When a kid is going through trauma, they will have a difficult time concentrating on their academics, and they will score poor grades. Also, they will have difficulties comprehending whatever they are learning because most of their mental energy goes toward processing the traumatic experiences they are going through.

- **Risky behavior**

In most cases, trauma tends to overwhelm kids and makes them quiet. But then there are cases where kids react to trauma by going over the board. Such kids will start indulging in risky behaviors as a way of trying to forget their traumatic experiences. Of course, such behaviors only prepare them for the path of delinquency and more often than not it ends badly.

- **Aches**

Some kids react to traumatic experiences through feeling pain in certain areas of their body. This can be especially unnerving because kids need to be in great physical health so they can enjoy their early childhood.

People who have insecure attachment issues are likely to have gone through a traumatic experience in their early childhood. It gets worse depending on whether or not anyone came to their aid.

Chapter 7:

Failure and rejection

A person who's struggling with insecure attachment issues might very well have a terrible relationship with failure. This usually means they don't know how to pick themselves up when they experience a failure and they end up developing attachments. Most people who are susceptible tend to have a weak spirit and they are bothered by the smallest failures they could run into. Of course, such a mentality makes their life terrible.

The following are some of the ways that failure might affect someone and cause them to develop insecure attachment issues.

- **Loss of hope**

Let's say that someone has graduated from college and they spend the next few months looking for work, and it doesn't matter that they have dropped their documents to hundreds of companies, but still they haven't got an opportunity. This becomes increasingly frustrating and they might lose hope for getting any work. Or, if they are not getting positions that align with their qualifications, they might think that they will never get their foot in the door for the career that they are passionate about. When a person loses hope they stop trying because nothing else matters. They think that the world is against them, and in the worst-case scenario, they might want to attach themselves to other people, in a misguided attempt to gain security. The fact of the matter is that people are responsible for their reality and one cannot escape their reality by trying to latch on someone else, for it has great potential of backfiring.

- **Inaccurate perception of one's abilities**

In order to shine and become the best that you can be, you first need to have the right mindset. You need to believe that you have what it takes to achieve greatness. In the beginning, when people are trying to break into their industry, they strongly believe in their potential, but as soon as they run into the first obstacle, it seems they start believing less in their potential. Most aspiring writers go through this phase. In the beginning, they are looking to get their script published, and they think they are a big deal, but then the rejection makes them think that they are not as able as they first imagined, and it causes them to develop unhealthy habits like attachments.

- **Feeling of helplessness**

In some instances, failure can make you feel as though you are helpless. It can make you feel as though you are head in the wrong direction and you cannot be helped. When you run into failure many times, it can potentially make you feel as if you will never amount to anything in life. And with such a negative belief, you start developing unhealthy attachments with other people, thus making it hard to become emotionally stable and lead your life on your own terms. The worst feeling that one can feel is helplessness. We want to always think that we are in control. Once we start thinking that we have no control, desperation sets in, and gives rise to unhealthy habits like insecure attachments.

- **Fear of failure**

Another reason why people develop insecure attachments is due to their fear of failure. They seem to think that they don't have it in them to succeed. And this mental conditioning makes it hard for them to try again and again. For instance, if you are a talented actor, and you go for a few auditions, but you are not lucky, it doesn't mean that your career is over, but rather you should try even harder and eventually the success will come. However, most people don't reason like that, for the first few instances of failure are enough to stop them from ever trying again. And thus, they opt for the easiest thing, which is to develop unhealthy attachments, hoping that the other person will hold them down because they are looking for security.

- **Self-sabotage**

We have the potential of becoming the best that we can be, but when we self-sabotage, we take away all of that potential. They are various ways we self-sabotage especially after failure. For instance, we might develop the tendency of magnifying even small issues, so that we don't have the energy to do the things that we want to do, and in the long run we are unable to develop the stamina necessary to achieve our goals. And this feeling of failure causes us to feel empty and we tend to seek other people in order to feel stable ourselves.

- **Increased anxiety**

Failure can bring bout anxiety. Anxiety, as noted earlier, is a perfectly normal biological force. But then this force becomes dangerous when it has a domineering presence in our lives. Some people develop insecure attachments as a result of battling extreme anxiety. They are in a perpetual state of worry, thinking about the next thing that could go wrong, and they resort to unhealthy habits like clinging on other people, so that they can be shielded from reality. Of course, such an approach rarely works, and in the long run they find that they have to work on their problems so that they may be well-adjusted.

- **Loss of motivation**

When someone is trying to get something on their first attempt, they are usually motivated, but when their plans hit the wall, this motivation could escape them. in place of motivation comes lethargy. They don't seem to have the drive or ambition anymore. What's the point of trying if there's failure around the corner? It's a twisted way of looking at life, but most people are exactly like this. With loss of motivation, people might find it hard to cope with day to day living, and then they resort to developing unhealthy habits like clinging on other people just to be secure.

Another major factor that usually affects people and drives them into developing insecure attachment issues is rejection.

As human beings, we are social animals, and we are incredibly sensitive to whether other people like us or are against us.

If we find that other human beings are somewhat opposed to us, it can cause us tremendous grief.

The worst kind of rejection takes place in our early childhood, when, for instance, our parents walk out on us, and we have to grow under single-parent households or we are taken to foster homes.

It leaves us wondering whether we were not worthy enough of our parent's love.

When we are adults, and we seek love from other human beings, and seem not to find love, it can also give us tremendous pain, and this could be hugely problematic.

Also, when we are looking for a job, and we drop our applications at various places that we qualify but somehow, we fail to get the job simply because we have no backing, this can also be interpreted as rejection.

Rejection can leave a major emotional scar. It can leave us feeling incomplete.

And in those moments, we are susceptible to develop various unhealthy attitudes, including insecure attachment issues.

Rejection has a subtle presence in our lives. The following are some of the ways that one might know they are still battling the pain of rejection.

- **Negative assumptions over other people's thoughts**

Since we have been rejected before, we might think that everyone is going to reject us. And so, when we are in a social gathering, we might find ourselves looking for evidence to support the belief that everyone is against us. People who are struggling with rejection will commonly develop negative assumptions about other people's thoughts. This causes them to have a negative attitude and it makes their fears come true. It might be that the other person wasn't actually thinking something bad of them, but seeing their attitude of negativity, it causes them to now dislike them, and want to have nothing to do with them; effectively making their fears a self-fulfilling prophecy. With such an attitude, it increasingly becomes difficult to have a relationship with anyone, thus making the fellow desperate, but finally, when someone comes along and expresses interest in having a relationship with them, they exhibit unhealthy habits like clinginess.

- **Wary about engaging other people**

Someone who's nursing the pain of rejection will be wary of opening up to people. They have a deep distrust for people. They seem to think that everyone is out to get them. And it doesn't matter who it might be, but they think that their intentions are not bright. Of course, when one has such a dark attitude, it draws them even further from well-meaning people, and in the long run, they fall in the pit of desperation. Such people tend to have a habit of testing people in their life, because they are always expecting to deal with the worst from human beings, and obviously it makes their life hard. In the end, they are desperate and they start clinging on anyone that might be around them.

- **Difficulty making compromise**

For relationships to be stable, people have to learn to compromise. You cannot have it all. You cannot always get your way. You have to learn to adjust to the wishes and demands of your partner. But then some people who are nursing the pain of rejection have such a hard time making a compromise because it grieves them that they cannot be allowed to be themselves and ask for what they want. People who have experienced rejection seem to think that the other party was disapproving of some aspect about them, and this is what makes them have even a nastier attitude. The inability to make a compromise obviously causes people to have smooth relationships and it invites many toxic habits into their relationships.

- **People-pleasing**

In most cases, rejection makes one recoil, hurt, and resent humans in general. Most people who have faced rejection in their life tend to have a negative outlook on both life and human beings. But then there's a class of people who interpret rejection as disapproval from people, and they figure that to win people's approval, they need to please them. Nothing else can be as self-sabotaging as having to people-please. It means that you don't have sufficient self-esteem. It means that you are weak. And it causes you to be a target for predators. When you have a tendency to pleasing other people, once you get into a relationship, it becomes hard for you to be happy, because you push back your needs and makes it about the other person. This façade cannot be sustainable in the long run. And this causes the relationship to fall apart as both partners are consumed with bitterness.

- **Not being good enough**

Rejection can leave one feeling like they are not good enough. It can leave one feeling incomplete. And as a result, these people could go looking for love from external sources. If someone doesn't feel good enough it means they won't trust their judgment. It means they won't make a point of chasing their dreams because they feel they have no chance of making their dreams come true. This pervasive feeling of not being good enough spills into every aspect of their life and sabotages their progress. And such a tendency pushes people into developing unhealthy habits that eventually eat away their relationships.

- **Inability to show genuine love**

When we talk about people with insecure attachment issues, it might seem that they are in love with their partners, but that's not usually the case. Their actions and thoughts come from a place of desperation and pain. For that reason alone, such people are incapable of showing their partners genuine love, which is sad. Rejection might cause an individual to have a warped sense of self and from there onwards the individual doubles down on the negativity, and in the long run, there's more heartbreak, unless they are willing to seek help and confront their deep-seated issues.

Chapter 8:

Negative people in your life

The fact is, there are more negative people than positive people in the world. So, when we say that one should try to keep close to positive people, understand that it is not as easy as you may wish.

But then the fact is, surrounding yourself with negative people can cause you tremendous pain, and make it hard for you to enjoy life.

Some people very well develop insecure attachment issues as a result of hanging out with negative individuals.

The most important thing about escaping the trap of negative people is to first raise your self-awareness.

So many people are not even aware that they are surrounded by toxic people because they have managed to deceive themselves.

But when you can understand that you are surrounded by negative people, and then make a point of getting away, it makes all the difference.

The following are some of the things that negative people would subject you to that ultimately contribute to the development of insecure attachment issues.

- **Pessimistic**

Negative people personify the idea of pessimism. They cannot expect anything good to come out. And they make it their mission to convince others about their pessimism. When you collaborate with a negative person, they will sabotage your plans, because they are always looking to dwell on the negative side. This mentality stifles the creative process because it encourages people to stop believing in themselves. Negative people are always happy to see plans fail and people come up short of their expectations. They are happy to see people giving up hope and accepting a mediocre life. And having resigned to such a fate, it becomes easy to develop various unhealthy attitudes including insecure attachment issues.

- **They play victim**

The negative person will also have a tendency of playing the victim. They cleverly execute this game so as to guilt-trip you. they are always looking to make you confused. They are always looking to make you uncomfortable. They know the buttons they can push. They know the various things they can say in order to get you guilty. But the intention is to hurt your self-esteem and bring you to your knees. They know full well that once they hurt your self-esteem it becomes easy for you to develop various unhealthy habits.

- **They are users**

Another way that negative people are trying to wreck your self-esteem is through using you. When they first come into your life, everything about them is all right, and it seems they cannot be faulted. But when they realize what you possess, they will always find a way of reaching their hand to grab at your resources. They know full well that by using you they will ruin your self-esteem. And this will make you an even easier target to pitch unhealthy habits and thus waste your potential.

- **Energy vampires**

When we talk of an energy vampire, we mean to say that someone carries a terrible energy about them, and they suck off people's energy. When you hang around an energy vampire you will feel your life force draining, and it's simply because this negative person is sapping at your life force. When you are drained of your life force, it means you have no energy to achieve your important life goals, and this conditions you to develop unhealthy habits just so you may get by, albeit pitifully.

- **They want to change you**

Being around a negative person can be a huge test because they will want to turn you into someone else. They have all the tools and a massive willpower. What's to stop them? They are scanning for people who have good values and then they will attempt to get these people to change their ways. They are looking to make people abandon their values and embrace the degeneracy. They know too well that if they get people to acquire a negative mindset, that is the seed of destruction, and the loss of self-esteem begins thereafter.

- **They ruin relationships**

The easiest way of ruining your relationship is by letting your partner come into contact with the negative people around you. Or simply letting the negative person have access to your partner. Negative people are not okay with people being in harmony. They are looking to break people apart. They are looking to destroy. And they are pretty much unashamed about it. When they learn you are in a great relationship, they come up with schemes to break you apart, and you don't see them coming. Agents of destruction. It's what they are. They can't help it.

- **Jealousy**

The negative people will always be watching you through their large green eye. They are sensitive to your progress. They hate that you have an advantage over them. They will resent you for having a better life for them. But it doesn't stop there. They will then try to get even with you. Their jealousy causes them to start scheming against you. Depending on the resources at their disposal, of course you will soon start encountering frustrations, and feeling as though you are fighting an unseen force. Their plan is to weaken you in order that they may suggest to you negative and unhealthy habits.

- **Gaslighting**

When you are surrounded by negative people, you will come away most of the time thinking that something is wrong with you. this is because negative people are great at making you think that you are crazy. It doesn't matter that you have your facts right. Negative people are far skilled in the art of twisting everything and making it seem that you are the crazy one. After hanging out with them enough, you start doubting yourself, and in the long run you allow them to compromise your beliefs. Negative people are looking to mold you into a negative person as well.

- **No empathy**

Negative people don't have it in them to put themselves in someone else's shoes. They have a rigid way of looking at life. they are vicious and unapologetic. They are cruel. But in order to become a well-adjusted person, you have to have a side to you that empathizes with people. In order to be in a stable relationship, you have to be someone that shows their partner empathy. But then negative people are preoccupied with their own needs and they wouldn't care what anyone else would be going through and they make it their job to make everyone around them become just as non-empathetic.

- **Hypocrisy**

When you are surrounded by negative people, the hypocrisy can be crippling. It would seem that they are always contradicting themselves. And this invites conflict in their life. negative people are not averse to conflict. In fact, they are looking for the next opportunity to enter a conflict, because that's their natural habitat. Negative people are two-faced and this is what drives their hypocrisy. They know how to carefully study a person and show them a face that appeals to them but that is far from who they really are. This hypocrisy, in the long run, leads to chaos.

- **Lying**

Being surrounded by negative people, you are never going to have peace considering that all of your intentions will be hijacked by their lies. You cannot depend on them. These people have a way of telling lies that you couldn't fault. But then the more you associate with them, the more you become comfortable telling lies, and in no time, you become someone who cannot be depended on. The thing about spending time with negative people is that they are looking to make you one of their own. But then once you cross over life becomes hard because well-adjusted people don't respond well to negativity. Stable relationships also require that the partner is coming from a place of good intentions, which is never the case when you are a negative person.

- **Criticism**

When you are surrounded by negative people, expect to be always criticized. It doesn't matter what you have done. It doesn't matter

66

what you are looking to achieve. But the negative person will always have an angle that makes it seem you are on the wrong. Of course, their intention is to break you, and when you pay them attention for long enough, they eventually succeed. Criticism can cause a person to think that something is wrong with them. it can cause a person to think that they are not going to achieve what they are after, and once such a mindset sets in, it becomes hard for the person to have a normal life. Thus, once you discover you are surrounded by a negative person, you had better step away from them.

- **Undermining your self-esteem**

Negative people are well aware that they only have to wreck your self-esteem and you are done for. They are pretty skilled in the trade of undermining someone's self-esteem. Since they have spent enough time around you, they should know the things that are dear to you. They know what they need to distort in order to wreck you. And then they will carefully start taking you apart, and before you know it, they are hurting your self-esteem. In order to save yourself that pain, you need to run away from the negative person in your life. If they succeed in ruining your self-esteem, they have pretty much succeeded in ruining your life, considering that nothing you can achieve when you have low self-esteem. Strong relationships require high self-esteem. Career success requires high self-esteem. And when you don't have any self-esteem, all your potential goes down the drain.

- **Comparison**

Negative people will try their best to make you feel bad about yourself. One of the common ways they achieve this is through constantly comparing you to other people. They know by doing so they will awaken your insecurities and send you mind on overdrive as you agonize over your perceived disadvantages. They are careful to portray you as lacking in one way or another, knowing too well that this is how they can get you to think less of yourself. When you have been compared with enough people, and your apparent inferiority is made apparent, it becomes far easier to break you.

- **Covert abuse**

Negative people will very well abuse you. But they are careful in the sense that their tactics are not obvious. One of the common ways negative people will abuse you is through devaluation. They purposely do this so as to ruin your self-esteem. They are also good at making you lose your identity so that in the long run you have no idea of who you are.

- **Arrogance**

Most negative people are good at pulling appearances. When you first meet them, they will seem happy and go lucky, and they will become friendly. But this is carefully done so as to make it possible for them to have a chance to learn everything about you. once they have learned everything about you, now their true colors come out; which is, they are impossibly arrogant. They have no respect for anyone. Such people will talk you down. And they will always try to expose you just so they can massage their ego.

- **Spread rumors**

Another beloved tactic of negative people is a tendency of spreading rumors. They are always looking to tarnish your name. they are well aware of the fact that by tarnishing your name and soiling your reputation, you will have a hard time in society, and it will ultimately hurt your self-esteem. Negative people know how to spread misleading information about you and make it seem like abject truth.

And whilst they do it, you could never guess. And even when you find out that they are spreading rumors, they will turn things around and try to come off as innocent. When your reputation is being ruined you are going to have a hard time building a good name, and if you are faint-hearted, it could easily break you.

Chapter 9:

Low self-esteem

When we talk about self-esteem, we are talking about your perception of self. People with healthy self-esteem think highly of themselves, and they are aware that they have the potential to achieve what they set their minds for.

People with low self-esteem think lowly of themselves. They think that they are powerless and at the mercy of the universe. They might have potential but they are not motivated for success because they think less of themselves.

For that reason, people with low self-esteem develop a variety of negative habits, under the misguided assumption it will help them cope with their life situation.

Insecure attachment is very well one of these habits.

Low self-esteem can be triggered by a number of things, but commonly it is anchored in negative childhood experiences.

The following are some of the behaviors sponsored by low self-esteem that can predispose you to insecure attachment issues.

- **Negative feelings**

To an extent, self-esteem is about having great emotional environment. People with healthy self-esteem tend to always be in good spirits. On the other hand, people who have low self-esteem tend to grapple with negative feelings. When you are experiencing negative feelings on a constant basis, it can become very easy to give up hope, and start exhibiting unbecoming habits. Negative feelings might condition us to act in an inappropriate manner. At the end of the day, it's all about feelings, and we are guided by what we feel like. Our terrible decisions are directly linked to our negative feelings. And our great actions are directly linked to our positive feelings. Thus, it is always a bad sign when you notice that you are struggling with negative feelings because it indicates your self-esteem is getting threatened.

- **Self-loathing**

Low self-esteem can very well cause you to loathe yourself. And when you hate yourself you are going to exhibit self-sabotaging tendencies. People who loathe themselves tend to let others walk all over them. So, it makes sense that they develop various negative habits that will help them cope with the self-loathe. When someone has a tendency of self-loathe, it makes them a target of ill-meaning people, considering they fit the candidate for someone who can be taken down with ease. Self-loathe normally originates from a place of unhappiness, or rather lack thereof, and the person journeys through life hoping to come into contact with someone who can take pity on them. And thus, people who loathe themselves easily pick up the negative and unhealthy habits, and this predisposes them to insecure attachment issues.

- **Thinking less of oneself**

It's amazing what a sufficient self-esteem can help one achieve. It can help one scale the heights of success even when they have average potential skills. But when you have low self-esteem, it doesn't matter the weight of your skills and potential, but you are likely to amount to nothing, because people cannot relate to someone with zero self-esteem. People who think less of themselves end up developing nasty

71

habits so that they can just survive. And this is the mentality that makes them ripe candidates for negative and unhealthy habits. They have demonstrated that they don't think too high for themselves and this encourages ill-intentioned people to step in.

In a relationship, people who think less of themselves will have no power, and their partner will always get their way. And this makes them even far unhappier.

- **Loss of motivation**

When someone has sufficient self-esteem, they think highly of themselves, and they expect they are going to accomplish their goals. This causes them to be motivated as they strive to make their dreams come true. Even when they run into brick walls, it never hurts their motivation, and in some instances, it causes them to actually double their motivation, and then they go at their goals with a renewed zeal. But when a person is suffering from low self-esteem, they seem to think that all hope is lost, and this sends them into desperation. When the despair kicks in, they are willing to attach themselves to anything or anyone just so they might feel a sense of security, and this predisposes them to develop insecure attachment issues. Loss of motivation can also affect the quality of life of a person. As human beings, we need to be productive so that we might earn a living. And when we are not productive, it means we have lost the motivation, and consequently, not in a position to earn what we consider sufficient, and with lowered standards of living, it can bring about its own set of challenges, and particularly, it can make you feel worthless.

- **Anxiety**

When someone has sufficient self-esteem. They know that they are not supposed to work like a robot. And this mindset makes them unafraid of trying. They are well aware of the risk of failure, but they never let it stop them from doing their best. On the other hand, someone with low self-esteem is first of all afraid of failure, or rather the implication of failure. And this causes them to approach their work with extreme anxiety. They will obsess about getting things right. And this denies them the chance to concentrate and tap into their creative mind so that they can come up with something truly of great quality. Their obsession with getting everything correct denies them the chance to utilize their full potential, and this is on many levels sad. Also, it is this anxiety that causes them to forsake the good habits and take up negative and unhealthy habits that are ultimately going to stop them from leading a happy life.

- **Inability to say No**

Most successful people will tell you that they have had to say No many times over the course of their career. Saying No doesn't mean you hate the other person, but rather, it is an acknowledgment that their request or wish is at odds with their schedule or resources. People with high self-esteem are not scared of saying No. This is not to mean that they say No for the sake of it. But if they are in a position to help, they will always volunteer. But on the other hand, people with low self-esteem will always Yes, even when they lack the resources to fulfill the request. This passivity becomes a huge attraction for predators. Ill-intentioned people approach them knowing they are suggestible. They suggest various unhealthy habits and the person gladly takes them up.

- **Low resilience**

There's a difference between being motivated and being resilient. When you are resilient it means that you never stop believing in a specific goal. You are not prepared to channel your energy toward other goals. And we see this a lot in people with sufficient self-esteem. They go with one purpose and if they hit a brick wall, they re-strategize and go again for the same goal. One person who's the epitome of resilience is Abraham Lincoln, who never let his personal tragedies kill his dream of leading his country. People with low self-esteem will move on to something else at the slightest hint of challenge that they encounter. They have a low fighting spirit. And this attitude causes them to endure a world of pain. Their low resilience predisposes them to various unhealthy habits as they try to carve their own path in life.

- **Addictions**

If someone finds reality too tough to bear, they start looking for ways to escape reality. And one of the means of escape is through addictions. People who are low on self-esteem will develop various addictions in order to get away from reality. Of course, this path is not sustainable, because one way or another, they will have to come address their reality or their problems won't go away. Such people get addicted to various things including drugs, alcohol, sex, and food. Developing an addiction makes it hard for you to have a well-adjusted life and sends you on the path of unhealthy habits. In this way, the victim is de-stabilized and they resort to various unhealthy habits, including insecure attachments, just so they might have sanity in their life.

- **Lack of self-care**

When someone has high self-esteem, they think highly of themselves, and this mindset encourages them to take care god care of themselves. You won't see such people running around wearing rags. You won't seem them running around looking as though they took their last showers ages ago. People with high self-esteem will always take good care of themselves. But then people with low self-esteem can very easily neglect themselves. And then you have to remember that human beings are incredibly superficial. We take things at face value. When someone fails to groom themselves, they start attracting people who are down on luck, who more often than not possess unhealthy habits, and the person with low self-esteem isn't likely to resist these habits. It is a case of attracting what you want to become.

- **Pleasing people**

It is okay to make people feel nice, especially when you have the resources and time. But then you have to draw boundaries so that you may have sufficient time to take care of your needs. People with high self-esteem don't go out trying to win people's approval. But this is not to mean that they are aggressors. They are simply okay with being themselves. On the other hand, people who have low self-esteem tend to be people pleasers. They seem to think that by pleasing other people, it can make their life more bearable, but in many cases they are disillusioned. Takers will always take. This attitude of trying to win people's approval means that they are easily suggestible and before long they have taken up negative and unhealthy habits, again disillusioned that these unhealthy habits will shield them from pain, except they actually make the pain worse.

Chapter 10:

Judgmental society

Society means a great deal to us. It helps us satisfy various emotional and physical needs. But then, society can also be the source of our pain. This usually occurs when we have to struggle with various things that society points out. Understand that society wants us to be uniform. And any deviation is unwelcome. But some people are just different, and it gives them tremendous pain to know that they are the black sheep.

Constant judgment by society might result in a person falling off the radar and developing nasty and unhealthy habits just so they might get by. For instance, they might be forced into relationships that don't suit them and get predisposed to insecure attachment issues.

In order to overcome the need to cave into society's judgmental tendencies, here are a few things that one needs to consider.

- **It's not about you**

When society judges you, it's not really about you, but it's about their perception. They are projecting their fears or limitations upon you. They are probably seeing their weaknesses in you and getting mad about it. If targets understood this, they would be much more at ease.

- **What matters is what you think**

As human beings, society is incredibly important, because it makes us feel part of something. When we have to deal with excessive judgment on the part of society, that's too bad. But then we need to understand that what really matters is our thoughts, not what society thinks.

- **Quit feeling the need to convince them anything**

Don't be the sort of person who's trying to win people's attention. Don't go around making people like you. If society seems to have a low opinion of you, just keep doing your thing, and don't bother about what's happening out there. Eventually, society will become used to you.

- **It's human nature**

You may not realize it, but even yourself you hold biases against certain things or people. Being judgmental is a human thing. When you understand that it is an instinctive kick, you stop feeling so bad.

But then again, it is important for an individual to have a clear direction, and a strong intent, so that they may not halt their progress.

Part III: Overcoming

Chapter 11:

Raising your self-awareness

Insecure attachment issues can very well stop you from leading a happy life. these issues can stop you from relating well with other human beings. And when you cannot have fulfilling relationships with other human beings, you might not be really happy. But before you can fight off this problem, you first need to recognize that you have a problem.

One of the first steps for overcoming insecure attachment issues is down to raising your self-awareness levels.

Self-awareness is an individual's capacity to comprehend what they really are like. A self-aware person has a deep understanding of themselves. They have a conscious awareness of what both their feelings and thoughts are like.

The following are some of the things that one might do in order to increase their self-awareness.

- **Know your strengths and weaknesses**

One of the reasons why so many people experience emotional turmoil is because they are not honest about their weaknesses. It takes a great deal of confidence to acknowledge that you are not sufficiently equipped to handle certain things. But this honesty is what helps you identify your strengths, and once you are playing on your strengths, you are in a better position to achieve your important life goals. Knowing your strengths and weaknesses is about understanding the things that you have a natural aptitude for and also knowing what you don't take to well. This understanding will help you craft a life that best suits you.

- **Ask for feedback**

It is also necessary that a person asks for feedback. The thing is, you cannot always know what you are like, because you really cannot take into account all the factors at play. But you can reach out to someone that you trust and ask them for feedback. This person should help you understand what you are really like. For instance, they can help you understand whether you are acting way too defensive, whether you are a people pleaser, or whether you are acting as if you are low on self-esteem. By having someone else study your behavior it grants you the power to understand what you really are like. And of course, this helps you work on areas where you think you are failing. In the long run, you become a well-adjusted person who's not looking to win people's approval and acting in a pathetic manner.

- **Develop your intuition**

Our gut feeling can be very powerful. It tells us a lot about the world around us. But in order to use this gift we have to practice. Most people have the capacity to use their intuition but somehow, they cannot come around to use it because they have gone for far too long without using it. In order to utilize your gift of intuition, ensure that you start with practice, so that you can become accustomed to your gut feeling. This ability will help you gain a deeper understanding of the world around you. When you have a strong intuition, it means that you will be in a position to read people, and this is incredibly helpful especially when you consider the fact that you need relationships – both personal and professional – with other human beings in order to become truly happy.

- **Know your emotions**

When you have a deep understanding of your emotional character, you are less likely to develop insecure attachment issues. You are in a position to understand the trigger of every last emotion that you feel. The more you gain understanding as to the nature of your emotions, the better placed you are to control yourself. But when you have no understanding of your emotions, and particularly, your emotional triggers, you give your power away, because you could be easily manipulated. Knowing your emotional triggers requires that you spend sufficient time going through your mental environment and looking for the corresponding external or internal activity. It is also important that you have conception of the various things that causes you to be ultra-emotional.

- **Set boundaries**

This is one thing that people with insecure attachment issues have a hard time doing. They cannot seem to set boundaries because they are all about clinging on the other person. In a perfect relationship, there should be boundaries, and this is because they grant people an opportunity to be productive. But when partners are clinging on each other's back, nothing productive can go on, and although it might look adorable in the beginning, in time the partners will resent each other. Setting boundaries is the best way of protecting your resources, especially time, and seeking space.

- **Self-discipline**

Another factor that makes it so hard for people to form stable relationships is their tendency to answer to their every need regardless of the fact that the environment is not suitable. By developing self-discipline, you are in a position to control your urges,

82

and this discipline helps you cultivate the right mindset. It helps you understand that human beings are flawed and you won't always get what you want. And you won't always be in a position to give what your partner expects. When you practice self-discipline, it increases your maturity, and makes you a better person, and most definitely a better partner. On the other hand, if you are the kind of person that answers your every need without caring about the results, you are inevitably going to clash with the presumably important people in your life.

- **Keep an open mind**

Another way to avoid developing insecure attachment issues is through keeping an open mind. Understand that we might acquire mental issues from our perceived inadequacies. And this is born of narrow-mindedness. But when you have an open mind, it means that you are not at all challenged by the stand of other people. You don't become insecure after hearing about what is going on in other people's lives. And being secure is an admirable trait in a person. It makes you a good relationship candidate.

- **Try new experiences**

This world has so much to offer. The world offers much more than you can handle. So, quit staying in your comfort zone, and get out to experience new things. The more you experience new people, animals, dishes, it will have a way of letting you know more about yourself. Don't be afraid of exploring the world around you.

- **Motivate yourself**

At the end of the day, there are either results or excuses. But don't be the sort of person who's always giving excuses. In a relationship, you will have your role to play, and you cannot afford to slack. You cannot afford to be a consistent failure. Motivating yourself will help you to become an emotionally and mentally stable individual. Motivation is about getting to do that which must be done even though circumstances are not ideal. Motivated people are not scared of challenges. The more you are free to take on challenges, the easier it becomes to fight away your weaknesses, ultimately upgrading you into an individual that wields power.

- **Meditate**

Many successful people have confessed that this exercise has been a tremendous aid to their success. Meditation can very well help a person attain a higher level of self-awareness. This exercise began in ancient times and it helps in clearing away negative energy from the mind. By indulging in meditation on the regular, you have the power to rid yourself of the negativity you might have absorbed from the world around you, and it helps you become a much better person. Constant meditation will help you gain mental clarity. And this means you are poised to make better decisions in both the personal and professional capacity. At the end of the day, the quality of our life is down to the decisions we make.

- **Keep a journal**

Another awesome way of increasing your self-awareness is through keeping a journal. This journal should help you gain deeper insight as to what is taking place both internally and externally. Record your thoughts, habits, and different occurrences. It will help you gain understanding as to what sort of person you are. And it will also help you realize the best way to fashion yourself. When you have a journal, you have the power to record your life as it unfolds, and it grants you immense insight into what you are really about.

- **Self-reflection**

This is the tendency to look back to gauge the weight of your deeds. It also entails understanding your motivations. By learning to view things objectively, to have insight, it emboldens your confidence and makes it less likely to develop insecure attachment issues. But when you behave like a loose cannon, mindlessly going on without any reflection, it can cost your emotional stability. Having the capacity to self-reflect gives you a chance to verify the impact of your decisions. It also allows you to clearly see what motivates you. Every person is driven by a particular motivation. But through self-reflection, you can truly understand the things that matter to you.

- **Question your thoughts**

In order to have a deeper understanding of what you are really like, develop a tendency of questioning your thoughts and beliefs. Don't just accept your thoughts and beliefs without checking to see where they are coming from. This will help you gain a true understanding of what kind of person you are. And the more you understand yourself, the more you will be able to play to your strengths, and you will have more power. When you question your thoughts and beliefs, it allows you to see the values and ideals that you hold dear in life, and it encourages you to become protective of them. If you have any values at all you will discover they are against developing unhealthy habits such as acting clingy with other people and suppressing your needs.

- **Examine your attitude**

Your attitude might play a role in the kind of life you end up having. If you have a great attitude you are likely to attract people with a great attitude and create a near-perfect life. But if you have a poor attitude, you are likely to attract people with mediocre attitude and create an unfulfilling life. Thus, it is necessary that you understand what your attitude is like. It will help you realize the need for an attitude adjustment. At the end of the day, a weakness of attitude is a weakness of character, and this weakness could deny us the chance to attain what we are hankering for.

- **Revise the effectiveness of your decisions**

Life is complex. You might think you are headed in the right direction, when you are actually lost. So, always take your time to weigh the effectiveness of your decisions. This is not to mean that you should grieve over your mistakes. But the importance of reviewing the effectiveness of your decisions is that it helps you minimize mistakes in the future. You cannot afford to keep repeating mistakes because you might run out of chances to right this wrong and get stuck with the consequences. When you have the courage to review the effectiveness of your decisions it empowers you. It also promotes confidence.

- **Exercise**

Another way to increase your self-awareness is through exercising. Our bodies are designed for physical labor. Sadly, our technological advancement has left us shifting most of the hard labor to machines, as we are left to spend the day in an office. One of the ways to counter the negative effects of spending entire days in an office is through exercising. When we exercise, we get the heart to pump blood around with more vigor, to the benefit of most organs, especially the brain, and this aids our cognitive function. Great brain health promotes self-awareness. You don't necessarily have to enroll in a fancy gym. There are many freehand exercises you could perform in the comfort of your home.

Chapter 12:

Raising your confidence levels

Insecure attachment issues make it hard for you to become a well-adjusted person. Such a person has a difficult time enjoying meaningful relationships with other people. One of the things that one might do in order to resist the pitfall of insecure attachment is to raise their levels of self-confidence. When you are self-confident you are strong enough not to develop insecure attachment issues. Confidence amounts to being comfortable with who you are and understanding that you are enough. The following are some great techniques for raising one's confidence levels.

- **Groom yourself**

Don't let yourself go. Ensure that you have a great look about yourself. When you are perfectly groomed, you will feel nice, and this should boost your self-confidence. People will recognize your effort into looking smart and they will become fond of you. Ensure that your rooming skills are sharp. Grooming skills not only improve your confidence but they also improve your creativity.

- **Think positive**

It might seem like an easy thing, but it's nowhere near easy. In order to have a positive mindset, you need to really apply yourself. Think about it. We are surrounded by too much negativity. And if we are not careful, it can quite easily become our default mood. But we need to exert ourselves in so that we think more positively. By entertaining positive thoughts, we give ourselves a chance to be confident.

- **Cut out negative material**

At the end of the day, our thoughts make us. If we are consuming negative things, it is obviously going to affect our state of mind. Thus, it is necessary that we eliminate negative material from our life so that we may have a chance to develop our confidence. most of the things that sell are on the negative side. And thus, we ought to have a strong resolve to shun negativity from our life, and only feed our minds positive things.

- **Be kind**

It may not be immediately apparent, but people are going through a lot of issues. Thus, kindness is always welcome. When you help people get through a difficult time, they are tremendously happy, but it also makes you feel proud of yourself, knowing that you are playing an important role in terms of eliminating pain from this world. Being a kind person will always make you have a huge support system and the day you are in trouble people will come out to hold your hand.

- **Preparation**

It is also very important that you are prepared all the time. You must not allow yourself to become docile and inactive. When you are prepared it means you can take on all the problems head-on without any problem. But when you are not prepared you will sink into a mess. Preparation will help you shine and win everyone's approval.

- **Have gratitude**

When you receive help from other people, don't make it seem as though it was obvious and expected, but rather, be appreciative. People with a heart of gratitude tend to be upheld as beacons of hope. They are superstars. People take a liking to them. and this helps them strengthen their confidence levels.

- **Positive affirmations**

In moments of internal struggle, when you don't feel great about yourself, overcome this nasty moment through the power of positive affirmation. These are short and powerful phrases that reinforce the belief that you are indeed a powerful individual. Through the power of positive affirmations, you will be in a position to increase your positivity, and it will help you attain even higher levels of confidence.

- **Seek knowledge**

Understand that by seeking knowledge you will have power in your hands. Don't tire of acquiring more knowledge so that you may be in a position to understand what's really going on in your life. when you feel that your confidence is affected, you won't just take it lying, but you will be in a position to understand what is going on through seeking more knowledge. Luckily, we live in the era of technological advancement, and this means we have access to tremendous sources of knowledge, particularly the internet. We have access to cheap books and even free blogs. We only have to make a commitment to consume these books and we will be better off.

- **Avoid procrastination**

One of the forces that makes it hard for people to make any kind of progress is procrastination. When we are procrastinating on the regular, it stops us from taking charge of our lives, and pushes us into desperation. The simple truth is that change won't come around unless we take action. But in order that we are proactive, we need to avoid procrastination. We need to be doers. Don't spend time thinking about doing what you are supposed to be doing. Instead, just get started already. When you are a doer you are in a position to achieve your important life goals and it solidifies your confidence.

- **Have a role model and mentor**

The worst mindset we could ever have is to think that we know it all. The fact of the matter s that there are people who are better than us. We should make a point of learning from them instead of striking on our own. In this age of the internet, you are free to have role models from all the corners of the world, because you can reach them quite easily. But even better than a role model is a mentor. This is an individual who will hold your hand and guide you through the various challenges you may run into. Ensure your mentor is someone you would want to trade positions with. They will help boost your confidence.

- **Speak with clarity**

If you are one of those people that mumble incoherently, that habit has to go. You need to start speaking up, because when you speak with a clear voice, you come off as confident. But when you mumble as though you are afraid of who might hear you, it looks bad on you.

- **Speak slower**

People who speak extremely quickly are more often than not suffering from anxiety and low self-confidence. They are scared. And this makes them spew out whatever they mean to say as quickly as possible. One of the ways you may increase your self-confidence is through speaking a bit slower. It shows that you have thought through your message and are not afraid of expressing oneself.

- **Make eye contact**

When you are speaking with other people, you don't want to be the shy person who's always staring down, as if wondering what to say next. You want to be that person who looks people in the eye. That way, you make a great first impression, and people are likely to remember you. Also, this habit strengthens your self-confidence, which means you are less likely to get trapped in insecure attachment issues.

- **Greet people**

It's a cold world. People have a tendency of being apprehensive because they don't know what to expect. But you have to be someone who approaches other people. Take the initiative and say hi to people. People will always respond in a positive manner. Apart from getting to socialize with people and expanding your network, this simple habit will go a long way toward improving your confidence

- **Assume an erect posture**

One of the things that send out the message that we are short on confidence is a poor posture. People who have low self-confidence will stand up or sit up with their shoulders drooping. And once the ill-intentioned people spot that, they make a point of approaching them, looking to push them into unhealthy habits. But when you assume an erect posture, it shows that you are confident and self-assured.

- **Take up more space**

Another hack for increasing your self-confidence is through taking up more space. It lets the other person know you are extremely comfortable with who you are. Most people who have low self-confidence are actually ashamed of themselves. And this causes them to sort of shrink instead of taking up space. And also, it makes them easy targets for predators.

- **Have a brisk walk**

Your walking style can tell the world a lot about yourself. If you have a sluggish walking style, with your eyes looking down, you will send the message that you are low on self-esteem. But if you walk at a brisk pace with your face held high, you show the world that you believe in yourself.

- **Smile a lot more**

Don't be the sort of person who's always frowning. It tells the world that you are lacking in self-confidence. Instead, you want to be the person who holds their head high and walks with a smile. Being able to smile a lot more you not only increase your confidence but you also draw people to you considering people are always looking to connect with those who seem to be having a wonderful time.

- **Indulge in your hobbies**

One of the best ways to develop your self-confidence is through indulging in your favorite hobbies. Hobbies give you a chance to reconnect with who you are as a person, and in this way, your self-confidence is reinforced. When you indulge in your hobbies you have a chance to let loose and calm the noise of your mind. Also, hobbies give you a chance to meet likeminded people who may help you get through your difficult times.

- **Exercise**

Don't allow yourself to be the sort of person that sits all day in the office, eating junk, and then driving home at the end of the day to eat some more and jump into bed. You want to be someone who's engaging in some exercises. Through exercises, you may be able to improve the blood circulation, and boost various physiological functions. Also, exercising allows you to lose weight and get into shape. Make no mistake about it. People are superficial. People will judge you basing on your looks. And thus, when you are in great shape, you will receive more admiration. Exercising will just do wonders for your self-confidence.

- **Get out of your comfort zone**

Develop confidence is not something you achieve at the snap of a finger. You have to work for it. One of the ways to improve your confidence is by challenging yourself. This means that you have to be willing to get out of your comfort zone. You have to challenge yourself consistently so that you might become a better person. By challenging yourself, you will not only build confidence but you will actually have the benefit of bringing achieving your milestones. For instance, if you are an entrepreneur, and you decide to get out of your comfort zone, it will not only build your confidence but it will also help you increase your profits and grow your business.

- **Set goals**

When we have a goal, we have a sense of direction. It is one of the best things that one could do in order to boost their confidence.

Creating goals allow you to increase focus and realize the very things that truly matter. Goals allow one to understand the various things they are fighting for and this discourages them from letting distractions get in the way. Apart from increasing confidence, this tendency of setting goals helps one acquire purpose in life, and reach their full potential.

- **Improve your social activity**

As human beings, we cannot run away from the fact that we are social beings. We need to have people around so that we may satisfy our important psychological and physical needs. People who tend to isolate themselves commonly have low confidence. They are easy targets for predators. But people who enjoy social activity with other people tend to be well-adjusted and they have a high level of confidence.

Chapter 13:

Surrounding yourself with positive people

The fact is that we cannot possibly go it alone. We need people by our side. But then the big question is: what kind of people?

We need positive people around us. But sadly, there's a shortage of positive people, and an overabundance of negative people.

When you go looking for positive people to attract into your life, it won't be an easy task, but the reward will be well worth it.

When you are surrounded by well-meaning people, you are less likely to indulge in destructive habits.

Some people who take up unhealthy habits such as insecure attachments might simply not have any support system in their life, and this predisposes them to emotional instability.

When you surround yourself with positive and well-meaning people, you have the advantage of companionship and people who cannot spot and call out your poor judgments.

The following are some of the common benefits of having positive friends in your life.

- **You smile a lot more**

It might not seem obvious, but one of the factors that drive people in desperation to the extent of clinging on other people is simply unhappiness. An unhappy person might figure out that they have the best chances of being happy through forcing themselves into someone else's life, and such a mentality is the origin of their negative tendencies. But when you have positive people around you, you smile and laugh a lot, and this discourages you from having to go around impaling yourself on other people as you look for love.

- **Reduced stress**

Let's face it; there's a lot of stress around us. Stress can stem from virtually anywhere, but it generally makes life unbearable, especially if you have no support system. But when you are surrounded by positive people, you enjoy their warmth, and you won't agonize too much over the stress in your life. having positive people in your life can help you get through your tough experiences. People who have no support system can easily break under the weight of their stress. Such people can very easily start approaching other people as a result of being driven by insecurities and they would act very desperate because they lack emotional stability.

- **No judgment**

When you have positive people around you, you can certainly trust them. Positive people make a point of understanding what you are really like. They hate having to develop conspiracy theories in order to explain your habits or beliefs. So, they make an effort to understand your motivations. In that sense, they are not going to judge you no matter what goes down. On the other hand, negative people are always looking to make people bitter. It's a thing about them. When you welcome negative people into your life, expect that they will point out various things well calculated to make you feel bad. Even people who have repeatedly said that they are unbreakable, that they couldn't care less about what some other person thinks, even such people really have their breaking points. The criticism could become too much and cause them to snap. But having a support system i.e. being surrounded by people who understand you can help you overcome your challenges.

- **Constructive criticism**

Having positive people around you doesn't mean that you have an army of loyalists who will be shouting your name to the high heavens as they sing your praises. On the contrary, it means that you have people who are willing to see you become the best version of yourself. For that reason, the positive people around you will always see to it that they constructively criticize you when there's need. This criticism comes from a place of love. It's because they want to see you become a better person. For instance, if you have been exhibiting insecurities in your interaction with someone, your circle can approach you and tell you that you are behaving badly, and that you need to behave better the next time around, or else you risk losing your power should you go into a relationship with the other person.

- **They help you grow**

When you are surrounded by negative people in your life, they are looking to get something from you. They won't stop until they get it. They have a hawk's view of what is going on around you, and they know how to exploit you. Most negative people are nothing more than users. But when you have positive people in your life, they are interested in making you a better person, because they recognize that if you become a highflying achiever there can be mutual benefits. For that reason, positive people are not scared of making contributions in order to make your life much better. While most negative people have the mindset for tearing people down, positive people have the mindset for building people up.

- **They always listen**

One of the moments when we need to have someone around is when we are experiencing hardship. We feel vulnerable. We want to have someone around so that they might help us handle the pain. But woe unto you if you have negative people around you. Such people cannot show up.

But when you are surrounded by positive people, they will answer to your cry for help, and listen to your problems. But even more importantly, they will try to offer a solution. When you have such a support system you are never going to hit your lowest point so that you go seeking for unhealthy relationships.

- **Improved confidence**

To a large extent, it is the responsibility of an individual to develop their confidence. Then again, when you are surrounded by positive individuals, they can help strengthen your self-confidence. They achieve this by highlighting your awesomeness and making you feel that you belong. You are going to feel more confident when you have a tribe that you belong with. The positive people in your life will cultivate an environment that permits people to open and unashamed of who they are. This mindset of being totally comfortable with oneself is important when it comes to developing self-confidence.

Chapter 14:

Components of a healthy relationship

Healthy relationships help us become confident, grounded and well-adjusted. But it takes work to have a healthy relationship with your partner. In healthy relationships, attachment issues are unheard of, and the partners are generally looking to help one another. The following are key pointers as to what a healthy relationship looks like.

- **Partners bring each other up**

Partners must have the mentality of helping each other out, not tearing each other down. Partners must always work as a team. When partners try to separate themselves, it gives room for resentment, and then they start to sabotage each other. The moment partners start working against each other, it's the start of the end, and they have minimal chance of ever salvaging what they have. Bringing each other up doesn't mean that you sacrifice your happiness. It simply means that you provide your support for the common good. Healthy partners will have no issues with being there for their partner for they recognize that they will eventually need help as well.

- **Embracing each other's flaws**

As human beings, we are flawed. We cannot didge that. We are flawed when we are single and we are still flawed when we get into relationships. In healthy relationships, partners don't call out each other for their perceived weaknesses, but rather, they simply embrace each other's flaws. This is not to mean that you shouldn't work to eliminate your weaknesses, but rather, it is an attempt to create a positive environment for the relationship, and it is far better when partners are always working to become the best version of themselves.

- **You can be yourself**

For some reason, some people think that it's okay to present themselves as someone that they are not. In most cases, these people are driven by insecurities. They seem to think that no one will appreciate their authentic selves, and they are forced to modify their persona. They are just cheating themselves. One might keep the façade only for so long. The worst thing you could ever do both to yourself and your partner is present yourself as someone you are not. In healthy relationships, it's okay to be yourself. It's totally okay to express your peculiar habits without catching judgment from your partner.

- **Respect**

In healthy relationships, partners have respect for one another. They understand that each one is an individual. They understand that they cannot control the beliefs of their partner. Partners won't fight each other over a difference of opinion or difference in belief. Having respect for your partner means that you are not inclined to bend them to your will. You recognize that they have free will and they have chosen to do as they wish. People in unhealthy relationships tend to experience unhealthy power shifts so that one partner wants to dictate the beliefs of the other.

- **No room for codependency**

Codependency means that partners rely on each other for their emotional and psychological needs. This kind of arrangement might be great in the beginning but it quickly grows old. Healthy relationships require that partners have separate lives. They need to have a life of their own that caters to a certain degree of their emotional and psychological needs. For instance, they need to have friends that they can rely on, and this will help them have an easy time during their tough times. Codependency denies partners a chance to establish roots with their friends. When problems arise, as they are bound to, the partner is in a tight spot, and such an arrangement accelerates their falling out.

- **Minding each other's needs**

In healthy relationships, partners are not selfish, but rather they mind how their actions are going to affect their partner. Partners must be sensitive to each other's needs. Such an attitude promotes closeness between partners. Such an attitude ensures that partners are not driven to sabotage each other. The falling out usually comes after periods of not minding each other's needs. Problems start to crop up when one partner isn't mindful of how their actions affect the relationship.

- **Appreciating one another**

In healthy relationships, partners appreciate each other. This keeps their love going strong. When we talk about appreciating one another we mean that partners take their time to acknowledge each other's good deeds. Appreciating your partner doesn't always have to be a grand gesture. You don't necessarily have to fly your partner out to exotic places in order to show them that you appreciate their good deeds. Some of the simple ways to make your partner feel appreciated include writing love notes, buying flowers, and taking them out. After all, it's the thought that counts.

- **Respect for each other's families**

When two people come together to form a relationship, whether they like it or not, their families are involved as well. For that reason, both partners must have nothing but respect for each other's family. Neither of them should think that their family is better off, because such an attitude would encourage conflict. One of the things that shows partners are respectful of each other's family is through constant communication. They must reach out to their families and engage them sincerely in order to find out how they are doing.

- **Intimacy**

For a relationship to stand the test of time, the spark of love must be kept alive, or else it's going to be painful. The best way to keep this spark alive is through being intimate with one another. It is absolutely necessary that partners are intimate. In the absence of intimacy, it might point to a disturbing thought, the idea that one or both partners are getting intimate outside the relationship, and this would lead to conflict. Successful relationships take work. Partners must be willing to create time for intimacy and to explore their creative side so that it never gets boring.

- **Honesty**

In successful relationships, partners are not trying to deceive each other, but they are always telling the truth. It can be hard in some instances to tell the truth, especially when the repercussions are far heavy, but even then, you must earn to be honest. Being honest shows that you have respect for your partner. Being honest means that you care about your partner's feelings. You might have to face problems when you are honest with your partner but it doesn't compare with the kind of trouble you would be in as a result of not telling the truth.

- **Have fun**

One of the challenges that most relationships have is continuing to have fun. In the beginning, things are normally fine and dandy, and the fun is through the roof. But then time usually draws the partners apart so that they don't know how to have fun anymore. Healthy relationships don't allow it to get to that point. It is necessary for partners to expand their avenues for fun. For that reason, they have to be imaginative, or else the relationship will struggle. They have to have a growth mindset.

- **Effective communication**

Many studies have shown that poor communication ranks high up there – along with infidelity and finance squabbles – as the leading cause of divorce in America. Poor communication encourages the development of tension and disharmony in a relationship. In the long run, poor communication invites distrust and makes the partners go against one another. In order to have great communication in a relationship, the channels of communication must be kept open. Once a problem comes up, they need to face it, and not just bottle it up. The tendency to bottle up issues only makes the situation far worse because it reaches a point and the pent-up frustration erupts, precipitating a nasty fight.

- **Making each other happy**

It never stops. Partners must ensure that they are always making each other happy. Some people take this to mean they have to shell out a ton of money in order to make their partner happy. If you have the means, and there are no hard feelings, by heaven do that! But then making your partner happy is more about understanding the various things that put a smile on their face and making them smile a lot more. It means being sensitive to your partner's emotional evolution and making necessary adjustments.

- **Trusting each other**

In healthy relationships, people trust each other. They are not putting an eye on the back of their head as they hope to "catch" their partner doing something they should not. If partners cannot trust each other, the relationship is pretty much done for. It is extremely important that partners keep trusting each other. In order to ensure that you don't get it wrong, ensure you get it right in the beginning, which means screen your partner well. Be certain that you can trust them. If they are putting up a front, the situation cannot be helped, because cheats will always be cheats.

- **Respecting each other's boundaries**

Being in a relationship doesn't mean you are joined to your partner at the hip. There needs to be healthy boundaries so that you may respect each other's time. Even though you are in a relationship, understand that your partner must have another life, for instance, their professional life, in order that their life may be whole. When you trespass on their boundaries you make it hard for them to reach their milestones and it is an indication that you don't respect them. in a healthy relationship, partners respect each other's boundaries.

- **Patience**

In healthy relationships, partners have patience for one another. They are not hostile. They are not looking to drag one another by the hairs of their head for small mistakes. They are royally patient with one another. If one of them asks for a favor and receives a positive answer, they understand that their favor will be granted, and there's no need to make a fuss over it. They have learned to be patient with their partners and to always look onto the positive side. In unhealthy relationships, partners have a militant attitude toward each other. If they don't get their way there's going to be war.

- **No jealousy**

In healthy relationships, there's no jealousy. Partners don't look at each other with the green eye, agonizing about how the other person has it better than them. There's no possessiveness. In healthy relationships partners are supposed to support each other because they understand too well that the victory of either one will be shared between them. They are not caught up in a power struggle to try to see who will dominate the other. When jealousy enters a relationship, everything goes to hell, because it begins to taint the motive of every decision.

Conclusion

Insecure attachment denotes people whose habits in a relationship are primarily driven by fear. As you would expect, fear contaminates relationships, and the partners have a hard time getting along. Insecure attachment issues are mostly rooted in childhood trauma. If someone grew up under parents who were not particularly loving, this could be the root of their attachment issues. When you have attachment issues, you are not in a position to seek out healthy partners, or create a healthy relationship for that matter. Insecure attachment causes people to exhibit various habits that inspire toxicity in their lives. Getting over insecure attachment issues, one needs to have a deep look into their life and be honest with themselves. Most people are not in a position to overcome their faults because they are trapped in the cage of self-deceit. So, unless one is willing to take a hard look at themselves and decide to make a change, they cannot be helped.